# Hello Mom
# Goodbye

## Holly Rhoton

# Contents

# Foreward

♥

## Trigger Warning

I'd like to first start with a trigger warning. This book addresses some of your deepest childhood traumas. I am not a licensed counselor, nor do I claim to be. I'm simply sharing my journey toward healing, and what worked for me, in hopes that it may help you too. If you've had a very traumatic childhood, it's recommended that you work your way through this book under the guidance of a licensed counselor. We're going to talk about some heavy stuff. There's no shame in seeking extra support.

Speaking of extra support, I always thought it would be nice for siblings to work through this book together. If you don't have siblings, that's okay. But if you do, maybe see if they want to embark on this journey with you.

Either way, this book is meant to be a guide towards healing. But healing hurts a lot of the time. If at any time it gets to be too much, don't hesitate to set it down while you process things. It will get easier. And you will get through this. As Glennon Doyle says, "You can do hard things."

\*\*\*

Your relationship with your mother may be different than mine. And that's okay. There's something for everyone in this book.

If your mom wasn't perfect, I got you. If she was an alcoholic, we'd likely have a lot in common. If your mom was the best mom ever, you'll still find value here. If your mom is still alive, you're even braver than I am, and I hope this book strengthens your relationship with her.

Whatever the case may be, I hope that you'll find healing within this book as I've found healing in writing it. I want to thank everyone who contributed quotes and insights to this book. Each of us has had our own experience with grief and it's been beneficial to give other perspectives a voice.

This book is for the children within us, the children of imperfect parents. You've lost more than a mother. Sometimes you've lost part of your childhood, or the option to be a child at all. You lost a big relationship that played a huge role in creating the human you are. You lost the future.

This book is a journey through the great, and not so great. It's a gift of understanding, and sometimes seeing your mom for who she really was for the first time. It's a gift of love, and of finding your own love for a mother who wasn't perfect. And it's a gift of healing for yourself. Healing more than your grief, but a lifetime of things that need healing. For you, the family that came before you, and most importantly, the children that come after you.

My mom was a real alcoholic. I don't know if there's an award or trophy for it, but if so, she would have won it. She was a "beer for breakfast" kind of drinker. She took beer on hikes, in the car, to work. She drank alone and with friends. Every occasion was an occasion to drink. She was famously drunk at the birth of her first grandchild.

And that's why she died at the not-even-old age of 59. Just weeks after a birthday she wasn't even aware of. And that's where it all begins really. That's where it turns into something real.

Have you ever had an experience so painful, you can no longer ignore it? This is pain stacked on top of years of other pain. Hidden pain. And that's where the journey begins. Where the pain becomes a living thing that must be dealt with, and where the journey towards healing begins too. When the pain gets so great, that you have no choice but to deal with it.

Facing these demons might be the hardest thing you ever do. But I think you'll be surprised to find that not all of them are demons. Some are just lost children, making mistakes without knowing what it will cost.

I want to thank you for reading this book. Not just because writing books is how I hope to earn a living, but because the world needs more brave healing. We need to stop running from the pain and turn and face it. If you don't, you'll pass it on to your kids. I was that kid, maybe you were that kid too. Be the adult that kid needed.

That's what this book is really about. If one person, just one, reads it and does some of the work in here, the world is already a better place. And that's enough. That will have been worth the price I paid to write it.

Facing my grief has shattered my soul, and then rebuilt me. It's hard and exhausting work. But the version of me that came out the other side of this was infinitely better. I see things now that I didn't before. I have a sort of sacred strength I didn't know I was capable of.

So, in turning this around to you, I applaud you for being brave enough to face this loss. It is in dealing with the grief that you find healing. Not dealing with the grief is the worst thing you can do. It just pushes the pain deeper, ensuring that you keep it, that it colors every other thing in your life. Unresolved grief only delays your spiritual, and personal growth and can have many side effects which we're going to delve into.

No one teaches you how to grieve. Our society likes to rush through grief just like we rush through everything else. Sometimes it seems easier to stuff it down than to look it in the face. But grief is a natural part of life. None of us will get out of here without having been touched by the hand of grief.

You are not alone. Your grief is my grief, and mine is yours. This is a journey each of us will face and we can face it together. Only those of us left behind understand the true cost of goodbye. But in goodbyes, you may be surprised to find some hellos. Grief often leads to more love. Allow your grief to lead the way.

Let's move through this together.

# *My Story*

♥

If you look into my dark brown eyes, you might catch a glimpse of the eyes that were mine as a small child. Brown eyes.

Through these eyes, I saw too much too soon. And perhaps things I shouldn't have seen at all. When you look into my eyes, you might see infinite choices. My choices and the choices of my parents. Choices that led me here, to become the human I am today.

When I look into my eyes I see a strong woman, but a woman who had to go through challenges to hone this strength. A woman who has been broken and put herself back together time and time again. I see all the should haves, would haves, could haves. I see it all. And I am this woman because of the challenges I've faced, starting as a child. I still see that child when I look in the mirror sometimes. This is her story.

This is the story of my life with my mom. The story of a girl who grew up and grew through having alcoholic parents. I needed to write this book for that little girl I used to be, for the adult standing here today, and for you. Because I wasn't the only one to grow up this way. And we could all use some healing. Even if now our moms are gone and it's too late to alter the course of history. There is healing in going back and then finding the way forward.

***

My parents were both big drinkers. Not the kind of people that liked to let loose once in a while, the kind that were always loose. From sunup to sundown, they were drinking. It may have started for fun. But it became something they couldn't go without. The party favor became the life crutch.

My dad died from alcohol-related health problems on May 15, 2007. I was 20. It was unexpected. We were all shocked. This was the first of many deaths that would come because of alcohol. Deaths that could have been prevented. It was the first death of someone close to me.

My mom lived on as our sole parent. That may be why her death hurt me so much more. Or maybe because I'm older and now understand what death means. But part of me also thinks it hurts so much because of the bond a daughter forms with her mom. Even a bond riddled with bullet holes is still a bond.

I can remember my parents, first together, and then separately after they divorced, drinking all the time. Every day.

It's hard to summarize a whole life in one or two chapters. But I'll do my best for you.

My parents had four children together, (but I have three more brothers as well). My mom was married four times. And through her love and loss and drinking, we were exposed to quite a bit. Because of that environment, I was wounded quite a bit.

One of my mom's divorces happened before we came along. My dad was her second husband and would be her second divorce.

My parents worked together, drank together, and fought together. They had parties. I remember big parties in the yard. My mom would spend days cleaning the yard in preparation.

Some of it was good fun. Like the chicken shit game. I'm not making this up. My dad would paint squares with numbers on a board, he'd fence the board off with chicken wire, and they'd borrow a chicken. Everyone would buy a square, and whichever square got pooped in first, was the winner. The owner of that square got the pot.

I remember mostly good times like that. They were a fun bunch. At least that's how it starts with alcohol. It starts as something fun. It's not until many years later, when the damage is done, that it starts to be a whole lot less fun.

While we were little this felt like running around outside, playing. We had freedom. We had fun. They made sure we ate, that we had clothes, and that our basic needs were met.

We didn't realize until later what was happening around us. In that way, it's easy to look back on this time with fondness.

Any time there's alcohol involved, there will be fighting as well. So, while most of our childhood felt like freedom and games, it wasn't always fun in the sun. There were fights between my parents and their friends, and fights between my mom and dad. Probably more than I consciously remember since I was so young. There were tears. And there was cheating too, since that's ultimately the reason my parents divorced. Or the final straw at least.

I was only around five at the time. My mom was already living with her new boyfriend, Dave, during the divorce process. He became husband number three.

My mom was a hard worker but always lived with men who could take care of her (and her kids).

When she left my dad, she met Dave. She ended up with full custody of my sister and me, while my brothers lived with my dad. We'd bounce back and forth sometimes but Dave's house became our home.

Some say Dave was the love of her life. She loved him with a fierceness. I think she loved him more than she loved herself. And because of that, she put up with so much more than she should have.

Dave was a spoiled only child. But he came from good parents. Probably something my mom wanted to be part of since she was raised by an alcoholic father after her mother left them when she and her twin sister were only babies.

She was especially fond of Dave's dad, JD. He was a sweet old man with a little bit of money. He bought my mom a Lincoln Continental. It was a sleek dark blue. It had automatic windows. She'd drive us down the road blasting our eardrums out with the radio. She loved that car. And she loved JD. She took care of him as he got older and more frail. She was kind to him, fed him, and even bathed him when he could no longer do it himself. She took care of him until the day he died.

She didn't have the same loving relationship with Dave's mom. She and my mom were very different women with very different backgrounds. My mom grew up poor, a child of an abusive alcoholic. Grandma Kate (as I called her), was an educated woman.

She didn't like all the partying they did. She didn't like the racy clothes my mom wore, mini skirts and tube tops. I think my mom tried to class it up a little around Kate, but she never could change her spots.

And so she and Kate were bound to clash. Kate didn't like all the parties either. She tried to reason with my mom and Dave, but it was no use.

Kate ended up living with us for a while. She'd take me out of town with her and buy me sophisticated clothing. She taught me the importance of good grades, and she inspired me to enjoy reading. I wanted to be sophisticated like Grandma Kate. So much so, that I'd read her romance novels after she finished them.

Let me be clear, I was much too young to be reading romance novels. I remember reading racy scenes and looking around the room thinking "Do they know what they're letting me read?!" But I just pretended that was normal and that I could handle it. I felt like a grown-up. I felt cool.

Parts of Dave were great. He was funny. He was smart. But now that I'm older I can fully grasp that the bad likely outweighed the good. He's not the kind of guy I'd want my daughter to marry.

I liked the house we lived in. A house that backed up to the forest and was on five acres of land. A big yard with plenty of space to play. Out back, I rolled old tires, one at a time, and stacked them up on top of each other. I'd use a tree stump to get on top of them and climb down inside the tube of tires. This was my fort. I'd stash my pens and paper in there, and trinkets and such.

Many times, I'd hide from my little sister in these tires when she came looking for me. It was my own private space.

My mom had built a big fire pit for gatherings in the yard. She was good at yard work. She had lined the outside of the fire with chairs, and beyond the chairs, there were stacks upon stacks of firewood she'd chopped herself. She had it frame the fire pit in a half circle. It looked pretty cool.

With the big fire fit, came big bonfires in the yard, and big parties. People were always over at our house laughing and having a good time. And drinking of course.

Around the age of ten or so, I got the bright idea to steal their beers and sell them back to them. I'd take one or two when they weren't looking and stash them until I had a stockpile.

There would always come a time when everyone was too drunk to drive. No one wanted to risk it. That's when I'd say, "I know where a beer is. Give me two bucks and I'll go get you one." I hustled a lot of money off of them with their own beer over the years.

Alongside the parties, my mom a Dave built a home together. My mom always made dinner and used to like baking. She wasn't the best cook, but she'd try. And she made some really good sourdough bread. I remember eating it fresh out of the bread-maker with just a little butter. She liked to provide for us in that way. She always had treats. Any time she went to the gas station, she'd bring us candy. Any time she went grocery shopping, she'd get us some sweets.

I wonder now if it's because they never had that growing up. No one ever bothered to get them treats.

But it wasn't all good times. They would fight a lot. More than my mom and dad ever did. And these fights would sometimes turn physical. I saw Dave grab my mom by her hair and slam her head into the corner of a wall once. She had a big open gash down her forehead. She should have gone to the hospital to get stitches. It was deep. But that would mean answering questions she didn't want to answer and would make her uncomfortable.

So she didn't. She had the scar on her forehead for the rest of her life. She cut her bangs to try to hide it. She was a vain woman, my mother. And she wanted to look beautiful.

Another time I saw him throw her down the front porch steps. I was at the bottom and saw her tumble down. I remember how shocked I felt at the sudden change, the sudden violence. While I'd never admit it at the time, I was afraid.

My mom got right up and charged after him. I think the friends that were there ended up pulling them apart. She wasn't as strong as Dave, but she didn't take it lying down. But she shouldn't have taken it at all in front of her kids. This pattern never seemed to change. No one learned from it. It just kept repeating.

Some of these things I've stuffed down so deep I don't remember them. My sister recently told me a story. One I vaguely recognize with a glimmer of memory, but for the most part has been suppressed. Dave had beaten the crap out of my mom one time. We were in the bedroom with her afterward and she could still hear that he was angry. So, she opened the bedroom window, helped my sister and me crawl out of it, and then we took off running through the woods. My sister remembers hearing gunshots. She didn't know if he was shooting at us, or up in the air, but he was shooting. And then a woman in a silver minivan picked us up and took us to a hotel for the night. They were back together the next day. And so the story goes.

Sometimes the fights weren't physical. Sometimes he would just say incredibly mean things to her. My favorite of these times was the time my Uncle Monte was there to witness it. Dave had said something mean to my mom and Uncle Monte didn't like it.

Monte was a left-handed drummer. He had killer arm muscles and long hair. He was the epitome of cool to me at that age. And he became cooler still when that left arm reared back and broke Dave's nose.

I remember Dave dripping blood down the hallway to the bathroom telling my mom who followed behind to help, that her brother had broken his nose. Which she knew, since she was standing right there. Uncle Monte was my hero that day.

Another alcoholic, one who probably had no idea how this was affecting us kids, but he drew a line in the sand. He said, "No one is going to talk to my sister like that in front of me." Ultimately, I probably shouldn't have seen that either. But I'd rather see a brother stand up for his sister with violence than a man beat the crap out of my mom. Even at that age, my brain could respect what Monte did. Sadly, my uncle couldn't be there every time.

I saw so many things a young kid shouldn't see. I saw my mom break down the bathroom door with Dave inside. He'd been in there a long time and wasn't responding to her calls. Of course, I was right behind her. I was always right behind her, watching, curious about what was happening. She tried to hide the heroin needle when we got inside and found him lying unresponsive on the bathroom floor. But I saw her sweep it out of sight. Even if I wasn't sure what it was at the time. That curious mind was always quick to see what others were trying to hide.

Dave didn't die that day thanks to the CPR my mom was frantically performing while we waited for the ambulance. I think by the time they got there she had revived him and he sent them away. I'm not sure how CPS wasn't called. Maybe they were good actors. Actually, I *know* Dave was a great actor. I remember he had such a charming smile. He could be so charismatic. Maybe that's why my mom always took him back each time they broke up.

One of those break-ups happened when we'd moved out of our hometown. She packed all her stuff up and sat outside in the front yard waiting for her dad to drive the five hours to come get us. Grandma Kate tried to convince me to wait inside. But if my mom was waiting outside, I was waiting outside. I wasn't going to leave her to suffer alone. I'd suffer with her. I refused to abandon her. My mom was fiercely loyal to us kids. She would never leave us behind. Maybe that's why I felt the need to stay with her in her suffering. A pattern you will see me have trouble with as I got older.

It should be surprising to me that I don't remember feeling frantic when any of these things happened. Panic would seem like a normal emotion in a lot of these circumstances. Instead, I just remember doing what we needed to do to get through the motions. A certified professional would say that's classic disassociation. And they'd be right.

I learned at an early age that you have to do what you need to do to get through. Worry about it later. Deal with this now. You can't break down crying. Or I couldn't at least. I had to hold things together for everyone. Any other oldest daughters here?

I very quickly became an adult as a child. There was no more time for make-believe. I needed to be serious. I needed to take care of things, and the people around me, since clearly they couldn't be trusted to take care of things themselves. Soon, I started taking charge in stressful situations. I became the mediator when there were fights. I tried to lead them away from fighting in the first place. I took care of everyone around me, (as the oldest daughter typically does).

I took care of my sister and my mom. What started as her taking care of me, switched to me taking care of her. I think she liked the idea of asking someone else what she should do. And soon I wasn't just giving my mom advice, but also other drunk adults who couldn't see how they'd gotten themselves into the situations they had. I'd blow them away with my intelligent words. But it seemed like common sense to me.

When I was at my dad's house, I'd take care of him too. He was around to cook dinner a lot, but much of the time he was at the bar. My older brother and I would make sure everyone had what they needed. I would clean the house, do the laundry, and start sorting things out and organizing the chaos that had ensued since I was last there.

I woke everyone up for school. I made (and drank) the coffee. I made sure we were at the bus stop on time, or in the car when my brother learned to drive. I was the voice of reason in the chaos. The one telling them not to do that and to try this instead. The one who couldn't understand how everyone else could be so carefree in this life. Why was I the only one who could see what the hell was happening? I was trying to instill order, order that would not come to pass.

I have so many unfortunate stories of my mom while she was with Dave. One time she left him because he was cheating on her. She found the woman he cheated with hiding in their bedroom closet. And yet, we ended up back at his house. She was crying. She said he wanted us to come back. She asked me what she should do. I told her I just wanted her to be happy. (I didn't say my advice was always good. I was a kid still after all). At the end of the day, it wasn't my choice. I was around 10. And I really did just want my mom to be happy.

So, we moved back in. This back and forth happened until I was around 12 when they ultimately divorced. With each divorce, my mom left everything behind. She never fought for the house or cars or money (not that there was a lot of that). She just wanted out, and her pride demanded that she didn't need a damn thing from any of them. Even though she'd been supported by each of them for the most part. After divorce number three, my mom moved us in with a different Dave.

Dave number two, her fourth and final husband. This Dave was nothing like the one before, probably on purpose. Besides the fact that he too was an alcoholic. My mom was tired of being hurt, tired of losing everything and starting over. This is the husband my mom had until the end. The man I consider my stepdad.

They weren't perfect either. There was still fighting and drinking, but this time my mom was in charge. Her name went on the title of the house with his for the first time. She had her own bank card, and her name was on the account too.

We always had a home. And I never saw Dave lay a hand on my mom. Instead of being a pawn in some man's game, my mom was the boss this time, and maybe to her detriment. The pendulum swung too far the other way. She'd spend all Dave's money. Most of the time it was on groceries unless he pissed her off. In that case, she'd spend it on other people or hotel rooms or a trip to the bar. She did whatever the hell she wanted in this marriage.

Because of that, of course, they fought. But by this time I was used to that, and it didn't turn physical, so it seemed like small-time stuff to me. The drinking continued. She'd drink and drink and drink some more.

Dave took care of her though. And because he took care of her, she was able to quit working and stay at home to watch all the kids my sister and I had.

My mom was the life of the party. She'd lost her driver's license after her second DUI and decided never to drive again. So, friends would have to come get her and take her out drinking. My sister and I would drive her to the grocery store or anywhere else she needed to go.

She always had somewhere she wanted to stop by. She'd take food to her brothers or go hang out with my Aunt Denise. Her friends, Loretta and Joyce would come pick her up to go out on the town. Sometimes when she was mad at Dave, she'd use his credit card to get us a room at the casino for the night. She would never leave us behind, so we'd get to swim in the pool and play in the arcade. Sometimes she'd swim with us and sometimes she'd be drinking at the casino bar. Well, she'd be drinking at the pool too.

Drinking was the main theme of her life. Her coping mechanism for living a life that wasn't what she'd dreamed. Over the years I slowly watched that coping mechanism kill her. She didn't put a gun to her head, but alcohol killed her just as dead.

She used to be able to drink a 12-pack of beer in a day and still be able to make dinner and function. But slowly, as she introduced shooters of Fireball, her body started to break down.

Suddenly, two beers would get her drunk. As the years passed, the life of the party started to be a lot less fun to be around. The woman who could walk anywhere she wanted, couldn't walk after a few beers. Instead of smiling and dancing, she was staggering and falling.

By this time, some of her friends had died: disease, cirrhosis of the liver, and drug overdoses (the first Dave eventually died of a heroin overdose). The friends she had left started to slow down. They started to feel embarrassed or sad for her when they took her out. They tried to talk to her about not drinking so much, but she wouldn't listen. Her twin sister tried to talk to her about it, but that didn't work either.

So, they stopped coming to get her. They stopped taking her out. Everyone, including me, started to distance themselves from her a little. Especially me. Her twin sister or friends would still come by the house from time to time. But most of them slowed down on that too because she always wanted to go out with them. My sister was the exception. I think she and my mom got closer during all this. But we'll talk more about that later.

She was recklessly hurting herself and ignoring all the alarm bells. It was extremely painful to watch. But even then, no one thought it would happen so fast. Until one day she was yellow. I mean, *really* yellow. I'd stopped by her house for something and couldn't believe my eyes. I'd never seen a person so yellow. Like a lemon.

I remember thinking I didn't want to deal with another issue with her. I was so tired of dealing with her issues. So, so tired. I told her to go to the doctor. She kind of waved me off like "Yeah, yeah. I'll get around to it." Her husband said he had made a doctor's appointment for her, but she'd canceled it. I told her she'd better get in there soon because this was serious. She said she would. So, I left.

As I was pulling out of the driveway, I was feeling a little guilty for not asking if she'd get in the car to go now. So, I called my sister. They were closer and I was ready for her to be the one that had to deal with all of the issues. I told her what was going on and to go check on her and see if she could get her to go to the doctor. She did. But my mom still didn't want to go.

A few days later, my sister had grown tired of arguing with her and called the ambulance. They knocked on the door and did what they could to try to convince her to go in, and *still*, my mom sent them away. She was so mad at my sister. She dug her stubborn heels in even harder.

At this point, we all started getting worried. Real worried. Everyone started to stop by to convince her to go. Me, my sister, my aunts, her friends, and even my brothers tried calling her. But my mom was the most stubborn woman alive. And she wasn't going to do anything until she was good and ready.

Where was I? I was at home, thinking it was time she started taking care of herself. Thinking I can't keep babying her. She has to fix her life or I'll be wiping her butt before she's 70. I didn't want to be in charge anymore. A lifetime of being in charge. I didn't want it anymore.

A week or so after finding her yellow, my sister tried to physically drag her to the car to take her to the hospital. She was pulling her by her feet trying to yank her off the couch while my mom tried to kick her. Finally, my sister gave up and crawled into my mom's lap and cried. She said "Okay, if you're not going to go then this is me telling you goodbye. I love you." That finally convinced her. She agreed to go. But not until the next morning after she showered and only with my Aunt Vicki.

My Aunt Vicki (my mom's best friend since they were seven) and my Aunt Tina (her twin) had to help her shower and dress that next morning because she was too weak to do it herself. She was much worse by this time.

Aunt Vicki took her to the ER, where they couldn't understand why she'd waited so long to come in. They started doing tests and giving her meds and fluids. She was transferred to two other hospitals. And within 12 days, she died.

Just like that, she was gone. Just like that, my siblings and I were officially orphans. Adult orphans maybe. But we had no parents, no grandparents to speak of, just Dave. And thank God, we had him. Honestly, we thought he'd go long before my stubborn mom. But life is always full of surprises.

And so begins the story of my grief and healing. And with it, your story of grief and healing. As we go through this together, I'll tell you a lot more about my life with my mom, what having alcoholic parents did to me, how their untimely deaths hurt me, and how I'm healing through it.

You'll read things that'll remind you of your childhood, or jog very different memories. While our stories may differ, the loss is the same. The pain is the same. Your pain is my pain, and mine is yours. Let's walk this path together friend.

# Many Kinds of Mom

♥

Did you know that every human has their own unique eyeball? Just like fingerprints, the pattern of your eyes sets you apart from everyone else.

No two are the same. Well, the two in your head are. But no two people have the same eyes. And no two people have the same mom.

You may be thinking, *'Well I have siblings, so that's not true'* -but it is. Each of your siblings sees the relationship with your mom differently. Each person gets a different version of your mom.

Maybe you complained that your mom was easier on your little brother. Or maybe she was tougher on him. She let one of you get away with more things. She held you to a higher standard perhaps.

Your mom's age and experience level when each of you was born were different too. The first child was new. She didn't know what she was doing. But by the fourth, she probably had a pretty good idea of how this worked.

Each child was different too. From birth order to personality, each of us is unique. Raised in the same house, but different. What hurt one child didn't affect another. What one kid found important, another dismissed entirely. You have different needs or desires compared to your siblings. And those needs were met, or not met, differently than the needs of your fellow birth-mates.

Each of you had a different mom.

In this chapter, I'm going to share quotes from people demonstrating the different kinds of moms they had, or still have currently. Many of these quotes refer to the pain caused by their mother since this book is about healing wounds. But some are beautiful too.

I had the great honor of hearing from these people when I called for help with this. They rallied and gave me what I needed. This is my story, your story, their stories.

***

"Not being close with my own mother, my grandmother is who I have always shared that (mom) bond with. She passed away in December of 2017. She was my best friend. She had the mouth of a sailor and told the dirtiest jokes. My GG had a voice that could mesmerize you, I don't care what song she sang, she always had a dirty version. She was full of life and wisdom. She always told everyone 'Fuck it. Just have fun.' She lived and died by those words. She believed that life wasn't worth living if you lived by the rules. She encouraged mistakes and embodied the wisdom of one who made many of her own.

She was blunt and to the point and would make you laugh no matter your mood. She loved using crude language to shock those who thought old women didn't know those sorts of things. She believed the smartest people had the dirtiest mouths, she thrived on others' discomfort at the use of bad language and enjoyed using them all the time if it meant someone would smile and walk away with a new perspective. She was essentially a less classy Betty White. She taught me life is a whisper that fades out too soon so we need to be loud and leave a mark. Regret nothing and breathe in every day and every moment as if it's your last." – Shaunie Lee Vandebogart

"My biological mom was someone I never wanted to become. Every life event, I somewhat congratulated myself for getting through the milestone and being nothing like her. Not making those life decisions and becoming the person she is." – Destiny Parades

"She didn't care what anyone thought of her at all. She was a very hard-headed woman with a lot of integrity. She was a single mom with 5 kids and she made it work no matter what. Even if it meant we had to go fishing every day to have dinner on the table. People called her crazy but really she was just funny and kind and loved all the kid stuff. She had her ugly moments, some took me a long time to forgive, especially after she passed away and were never addressed. But at the end of the day, she was my mom and I wouldn't have had it any other way." – Crystal Jennings

"My mother belittled, criticized, and never showed love or said she loved me. I've had to deal with scarring, guilt, self-worth, shame, and fear. When she died, I was left with all that pain, no apologies, and so many unanswered questions as to why and what happened to her to make her so mean and evil." – Sharon Storms

"My Mom, LITERALLY, saved my life. She was the only person I knew I could be honest with and not get judgment, no matter how insane I was.

Also, a direct quote from her: 'I don't believe anyone goes through life without thinking about suicide at least once.' – Marilynn Pejchl. (P.S. – I have yet to find someone who has disagreed with that statement.) She's been gone since December 26, 1990." –John Pejchl

"It's hard to understand unconditional love when all you've ever known is that a mother's love has conditions." – Kendra Alsterberg

"Growing up with a mom who was a drug addict, bipolar, and who also liked to drink was not easy. I didn't really trust adults growing up, and it made me independent. So much so that even when I know I need help, I still wouldn't ask for it. I struggled a long time to learn to trust people and learn how to ask for help when I needed it."

– Mandi Wheeler

"My relationship with my mom is best described as a tenuous truce. There are times when we're like oil and water and it can feel incredibly toxic between us. Other times I think we're on our way towards healing and understanding. There is a lot of bad history that often goes unspoken, and current ideas and thoughts that just tender the flames of the distance I keep between us for my own mental health and well-being. I love my mom, and would never purposefully hurt her, which is why so much history and resolve stays unspoken." – Tiffany Fleckenstein

"My mother tries to re-live being a parent through my children (her grandchildren). She even encouraged my kids to call her mom and to call me by my name instead of mom. She refuses to look at the past. She'll either say that I remember it wrong, that it didn't happen at all, or that she shouldn't be judged for the past. She refuses to face the hurt she's caused. I think respect between us is a very large obstacle. She believes that she's right and nothing I do or say will change that. I try to accept her for who she is because I can't change her or even talk to her about what bothers me. I can't spend long with her before things go south. I can't bring up sensitive subjects. But I maintain a relationship with her because I love her and so do my kids. But I can't say that it's always healthy. I just have to deal with her instead of having a real relationship with her." – Anonymous

"People think that financial success, having a family of your own, owning a house, or anything worldly that looks impressive to society is what's important. But my mom taught me more important things, like compassion, love, strength, to be accepting, and forgiveness – things that will matter once we are long gone." – Toria Graham

"A mother is supposed to be our safe space. However, it is now the place I find the deepest heartache." – Anonymous

"My mom was a hypochondriac that was addicted to pills. She was known as the town's crazy lady. She was high all the time and dated multiple men at once so her bills would be paid. But the worst thing she ever did was continue to date a guy for years because he paid her bills, all while he was molesting me. She just didn't seem to care until years later. I hated my mom for a long time and didn't speak to her. Much of the way my mother was, contributed to the suicide of my little brother. It broke me. But that's when I started talking to my mom again. She passed away suddenly, 8 months after my brother. Soon after that, my dad died too. And after a DNA test, I found out my dad was never my biological father. It hurt me that she could do that to me and I was so mad. But I've learned to move on and live my life." – Jane

"My mom wasn't good or bad. She was just mom
to me. She was a present mom who attended
parent-teacher meetings, concerts, etc. But she
was mentally ill. If we had friends over, it meant
we didn't love her. If we went to hang out with
friends instead of staying home, she would wish
she was dead. When I was five or six, my mom
slammed my hand in the car door. She said it
was my fault and that my hand shouldn't have
been there. By the age of 11, I was taking care
of my mom. I was raising her. It wasn't until my
now husband told me this wasn't normal, that
I realized the truth. I thought I had a normal
childhood. Today, I have no love for my mom.
I hardly visit. People tell me I'll miss her when
she's gone, but I won't. She is my curse, and I
am stuck caring for her and dealing with things
I shouldn't have to because she doesn't want to."

– Amber Pryor

"Sometimes the one person that you think you
can trust to love you and care for you turns on
you due to mental illness and will try to take

away the people who really do love and care." –
Lisa Atchley

"My mom would take my prized possessions
from me. She would even throw away books
borrowed from the library. When anything happened in our lives, she would shift the blame
to me. She allowed my brother to be abusive to
me. I never had a voice. Because of the relationship I had with my mom, I have trust issues,
I spent time being promiscuous, trying to find
love, or seeking approval. I don't think I ever felt
loved until I met my mother-in-law." – Maryann
McArthur

"My relationship with my mother was terrible
because she didn't care about me. I was her
punching bag for all her stress. I spent most of
the time hiding when I was young, which I think
is what makes me guarded as an adult. – Jason
Lamar

Some moms seem to do it all perfectly. They do all the things mothers "should" do. They cook, clean, show up for the PTA, chaperone the field trips, read to you at bedtime, counsel you, soothe you, comfort you, and take care of you when you're sick. They live and breathe for their kids. And that's fantastic.

Other moms appear to do it all wrong. They fall short everywhere. They aren't there when you need them. They never gave you a bedtime, they're too busy dealing with their issues to bother with yours, and maybe they didn't even care. Maybe you never had a mom. Maybe she abandoned you.

We all had different moms. And while I can't speak directly to your specific experience, I can share the experience I had in hopes it might help you heal in the ways I've healed.

My mother was incredibly loving. She truly loved us with all of herself. But she didn't do it all "right". She didn't have it all figured out. In some ways, she let me down.

Whether your mom was good or bad, there will be ways she let you down. Like my mom let me down. She loved me, but she still let me down. In the same way, no matter how great a parent you are, you'll fail your kids too.

I don't say that to be all doom and gloom, but the truth is, we're all human. That's one big thing I learned through this process. None of us are perfect. We all seem to know that, but to see it play out with my kids, and with eyes that have lost both parents, is something else.

Whatever the wound, great or small, there is healing in this book. There were things your parents couldn't give you. I've come to know that you can give them to yourself. You can learn the tools you need and grow past this. It's not over.

It'll take bravery to read this book all the way through. Real bravery. To delve into the pain that's taken up residence within you. It'll take courage to walk with it, explore it, and heal it. I'm telling you my story, but you'll be brought into your own in the process.

You're not alone. I'm walking this with you. I'm facing my pain, too.

Even after doing all the healing work within this book, you'll still have moments of pain. Some of it never leaves completely. But the pain will be different. Altered. It will be coated with love and understanding that you didn't have before.

The purpose of this book isn't to erase all pain. It's to heal it enough that it doesn't feel so heavy. Unpack the bags and just carry the parts you need. Leave the rest behind.

The person your mom was, has affected you, for better or worse. The story has already been written. But the ending can always change. The perspective can always shift.

I cried endless tears writing this book. I don't regret a single one of them. While it hasn't been an easy process, I've found so much beauty and healing in it. And I hope you do too.

I started this book angry at my mom. I started this book in big pain *because* of her and also *for* her. But through this adventure into my soul, I've found compassion. I've found love for her. Different than the love I had before.

In doing so, I've found a way to honor her memory, and love the human she was, instead of the human I wished she had been.

My grief was heavy. But now it's lighter. Now it's a friend that walks beside me instead of a weighed-down suitcase I had to drag behind. That's my hope for you while going through this book. In the many faces of our mothers, you might become friends with your grief and allow it to walk beside you too.

# A Mother Shapes Your Life

♥

"Her mistakes made me who I am today." – Moriah Taylor

The relationship you had, or didn't have with your mother has contributed to who you are as a human.

As a daughter grieving her mom, I've become fascinated with the mother-daughter dynamic. Of course, I never gave it much thought before my mom died. I took our relationship for granted. I was hard on her. In some ways, she deserved that. I can see now that much of my hardness was self-protecting behavior. Of course, on the flip side of that, I was blind to the reality that she would someday be gone.

Even though somewhere in the back of your mind you might know you don't have forever, you don't see it. You have blinders on. You assume there's plenty of time left. You try not to think about it. Thinking about it would make you sad, and we'll do anything to avoid feeling sad.

So, you don't think about it. Until you run out of time. This ticking down of the clock can be sudden, or it can go on for months or years. But either way, the time left is suddenly right there in your face. And the time left, is never, never, enough.

After the death of your mother, you may find yourself taking a closer look at the relationship you had with her. It suddenly feels like you're looking at it with new eyes. At first, you can't see through the confused mess you're left with. But as the excruciating pain in your heart starts to heal, you begin to see things a little more clearly. You begin to analyze the ways your relationship with your mom has both strengthened you and messed you up.

No matter what your relationship with your mother was, there's still love there. And no matter the *result* of that relationship, your mother helped shape you into the person you are today. Maybe she did that by not being there at all. Or by losing her before she ever died. We face loss through death, but also by leaving and being left.

Maybe she shaped you by being there too much or any varying degree between. But shape you she did.

Now with my kids, I feel like I get to see parts of myself re-incarnated. They're different people than I was. But it's like you're seeing a new version of yourself with different and hopefully better possibilities. You know what they'll face. You know what it's like to grow up. So you want to prepare them and help them. Not only that, in having kids, you get the chance to heal some of the things you encountered with your mom (or parents in general). You get the chance to do things differently.

You'll probably repeat patterns your mom passed down without realizing it. As you begin to pay more attention, you'll start to catch yourself doing it. The beautiful thing about noticing the patterns is that once you can catch them, you can change them. You want better for your kids. To give that to them you'll have to seek healing within yourself so you don't pass it on.

While raising kids, you can remember what you were like, what you needed, what you didn't get enough of, what hurt, and what left scars. You get a cheat code in a way. You have some research to base your parenting on. That research might only tell you what not to do, but it's knowledge to be used to better the lives of those who come after you. It's a circle, this healing.

My mom was the feminine energy in my world. She taught me about nurturing. She taught me about love. Dads teach you more about danger, about fixing things, about strength, rules, and consequences.

A mother teaches you the softer things. Things you can't see, but can feel. It's not weak to be soft. It's brave. It's trusting your divine femininity.

They don't teach you about femininity in school. And sometimes the things they do teach you aren't enough to navigate this world. My mom's education wasn't complete. She didn't finish high school and had no one to teach her about life. She was teaching from a textbook with missing pages. But she was teaching what she could.

Most of what she taught me wasn't through words she said. She found it hard to talk to us about some of the tougher topics. It felt awkward. I don't think she understood much of it herself. But she taught me about femininity and what it means to be loving.

I'd see my mom comfort me or someone else, and it made things better. Just knowing someone cared. Even if she didn't know what to say or have great advice, she cared.

My mom wanted to feed everyone. If you came over, she was feeding you. The kids had their own snack cupboard that was always stocked. There was always food in the fridge she could whip up for you and it made her feel good to do it. She might have been drunk while she was doing it, but she still wanted to do it. She gave people more than food, she gave them love.

She appreciated the outdoors. She had a serenity about her when she was outside. She always told us to be kind to one another and to love each other. She valued family and made sure it was important. We learned that because we could see how beautiful it was. Not to say that was always easy in this family. It would be much easier not to love each other sometimes. But at the end of the day, we do love each other. More than a lot of other families. I'd encounter families that do it all "right" that still didn't have love like we did. That was one thing we nailed.

Anyone who knows what it feels like to not be cared for can understand the importance of having someone to care for you. And maybe in your experience, your mom wasn't good at that stuff. Maybe she wasn't loving or nurturing at all.

If so, that likely shaped you differently. It made it harder for you to hug others or give or receive love. And yet again, mothers are teaching you about love. Either by demonstrating it or by the lack of it.

My mom used to watch Lifetime movies almost every day. I'd come over and she'd be sitting on her couch, tears streaming down her face. I'd ask her, "Why do you do this to yourself?" and she'd say, "Because it's beautiful."

My relationship with my mom was a dichotomy of good and bad. There were such beautiful things about her. But she was also a severe alcoholic that screwed a lot of things up. She was a mess, but that wasn't *all* she was.

Your mom teaches you who you are. From an early age, you start to see yourself as your mom sees you. That's how you first create an identity. I was her "smart child" and so I see myself as smart. But I wasn't her "beautiful child" so I didn't feel beautiful. So you see, this can be a double-edged sword. Your self-esteem and your actual self-image are shaped by who your mother thought you were and how she treated you.

Before we know anything else, we know to look to our moms for guidance. And so, the tone is set for our self-perception. If she's proud of you, you're proud of you. If she treats you as someone worthy of love, you feel worthy of love. Likewise, if she treats you as someone who can never do anything right, you feel as though you do it all wrong. If she treats you as worthless, you feel worthless.

For better or worse, your mother shapes your foundation. Sometimes it's shaped by showing us the people we wish to be, and other times it's shaped by showing us the people we don't want to be.

That doesn't mean it's set in stone. "This is who she thought you were and now you'll be that person forever." No. As adults, we get to unlearn the things we want to change. We get to grow and become the people we want to be, despite the humans we were molded into initially.

The purpose of this chapter is to understand the role your mother played in shaping who you are. To understand how it works.

Now that you have that basic understanding, I have a little exercise for you. Take out a piece of paper, or journal, or open up a blank Word document (whichever is the easiest or most comfortable way for you to write).

I'd like you to write a letter to your mom. In the letter, I want you to tell your mom all the ways she influenced who you are today. Share with her what you think she thought of you and the traits you now carry because of her. I've written my own letter as an example below.

*Dear Mom,*

*It's been a while. There's a lot I want to say, and by the end of this book, I hope to have it all out. But to start, I want to tell you who I am because of you. The good and the bad. Who did you think I was? Who did you treat me like?*

*Well, you thought I was smart. You thought I was brilliant. I could come home and do my homework without help, and get good grades without much effort. I think you thought I was a miracle. You treated me like I was smart. Hell, you even started asking me for advice. You knew I'd get good grades and you could count on that with me.*

*You thought I was independent. While maybe I felt I had to be to protect myself. You didn't ever act like you had to worry about me. You felt like I had it figured out, even when I didn't.*

*And you thought I was strong. I'm not sure you thought I was as strong as you thought you were. But you knew I'd live through all that happened and you dying. I think beyond that, you even knew I'd be strong enough to help everyone else through it.*

*I think you also thought I was an asshole sometimes. (I was). Sometimes I was mean and mad. I had a right to be. And because you knew that, I think you let me be a jerk to you when you maybe shouldn't have.*

*I think you loved having a daughter. I was your first little girl. You were excited to have me. You wanted me. I felt wanted. I felt important.*

*I felt like both a good and a bad daughter. And I think you probably thought all those things about me at varying points in my life and yours.*

*I think because I was smart, you thought I had it all together. You thought I knew how to do this whole "life" thing. And you couldn't relate to me a lot of the time. Because I knew more about things than you did. Not like I knew it all. But I knew how things worked or why I should or shouldn't do something. Things you had struggled with forever. And I wanted to be different than you. I didn't want to be like my mom. I wonder what that felt like. Not good. And it makes me sad to think about it now.*

*I think you assumed I felt like I was better than you. In some ways, I did think that. But I feel bad about that too. Not for doing better in life, but for making you feel that way.*

*You treated me like I was a good mom. Like I was a good person. A responsible person. But also like I wasn't a beautiful woman. You didn't think I was ugly, but I wasn't the pretty daughter. And I felt that from you.*

*I think I have a lot of good and not-so-good traits because of you. Because of what you did right and what you did wrong.*

*I am strong, but sometimes I'm hyperindependent. I have a hard time asking for help or taking it. I don't trust people. I want to control everything, and then get resentful for having to do everything.*

*I'm a flight risk in relationships. Leaving the relationship always seemed like the answer from where I was watching you. I didn't see any good outweighing the bad. So why would you stay? And why would I?*

*But I love hard too. I love everyone, even the people that hurt me. You gave me that big heart of yours. I know what it feels like to be loved that way, and that's how I want others to feel with my love.*

*Sometimes I'm stubborn like you. Or because of you. I had to be.*

*You were bad with money, so you didn't teach me to be better than you. And I sometimes feel like I can't do it on my own without the help of a man. Because that's what you showed me. I never saw you without a man. You always had a man to help you. Who would you have been without one?*

*Because of you, I'm understanding of people that don't have it together. I have a soft spot for them. Even though my boundaries around it get stronger all the time.*

*Because of you, I'm a pretty good human. You raised a pretty good daughter. You raised a daughter with some wounds she doesn't even fully realize as well. If I can't even remember all the stuff that happened, can I still heal all of it? I hope so.*

*Because of you, I am a damn good mom. And I'm always striving to work on myself, to get better, to heal what hurts, and to lean in and do the hard things. Because of you, I am a wounded warrior. Full of both good and bad attributes. But I'm doing my best.*

*Despite the bad, I miss you, Mom. And I wish you were here.*

*Love Always,*
*Holly*

That was the first of several powerful steps you'll take in this book. You're just now opening yourself up to some of that real healing and grieving. Don't run from it now. The first time is often the hardest.

I would imagine some things came up that you weren't expecting. That's what happened to me. There were things I felt or blamed her for that I didn't realize.

This is the first step in beginning to understand the relationship you had with your mom. You're going to be re-introduced to your mom. The mom you never actually knew. And that's the beautiful (even if it's painful) part.

# The Pain of Losing Your Mom

♥

> "There is something about losing a mother that
> is permanent and inexpressible – a wound that
> will never quite heal." – Susan Wiggs

In the same way your mother's life shaped you, so will her death. It's her final act of raising you. She delivers you to the precipice of real adulthood, where you're the parent now, the one to look to for guidance.

Losing a mom is a different kind of pain. I've lost my dad, the woman I consider my grandma, an uncle, friends, and other family members. At 37 that's a pretty extensive list. But losing my mom hit differently. Losing your mom is a different kind of pain.

She was the first love you knew, from inside her belly. Of course, you don't consciously remember that, but it's true nonetheless. She was likely the first to hold you, to feed you, to nurture you. The first to love you before you were even born.

Your mom dying is more than just your mom dying. It's her perception of you dying too. Her confidence in you. Her love for you. While all those things may still be true, the person who projected them at you is gone. Some say you're loved ones are never really gone. But she's not here where you can see her, touch her, have an active conversation with her. It's different now. And it hurts.

Because your mom influenced how you saw yourself, you may feel confused about how you see yourself now. You may feel a loss of identity. It's going to take some time to figure all that out. Be patient with yourself and know that it gets better.

You'll find yourself. Your feet will touch the ground again. The pain may never fully disappear, but you'll find a way through it. If the pain disappeared, so would all the beautiful memories tied to it. The memories are the reason it hurts.

This is a quote about that that I love:

"There is no death, daughter. People only die when we
forget them. If you can remember me, I will be with
you always." – Isabel Allende

I will always remember my mom, so she is always with me in a way. Even so, there's a unique set of circumstances and emotional baggage to go through. To love her, I had to first be mad at her. I had to be mad for who she wasn't and who she was. I had to deal with all that extra stuff to get to the love.

When dealing with the pain of losing your mom, you're dealing with the pain of losing your tether to the world. Like a balloon whose string has been cut, you feel adrift. Your feet are no longer on solid ground. There's nothing to grab hold of, you're floating up and up, and you don't know how to get back down.

That is what it means to lose a mother.

Even when the relationship was strained. Even when she was sick for a while and she's no longer in pain. It still hurts desperately.

Despite my mom's flaws, she was my biggest cheerleader. She had more faith in her kids than we did in ourselves. She was so proud of us. And now there isn't a person in this world that loves us in that same way. There is no longer a person on this earth that loves us unconditionally. No matter what we do, what we say, how we hurt her, she would never stop loving us.

I'm sure wherever she is, she loves us that way still. But to have that visual representation taken away is quite a loss.

There's also a loss of security.

"What do you mean I'm the *adultiest* adult now?"

There's just something about having someone else you can call, who's been alive longer than you, who's been a parent longer than you. Even if they weren't the best parent. There's something about it that gives you a sense of security. It's comforting.

I never really called my mom for advice. I always thought I knew better anyway. But now that I can't, I wish I could. And I don't know about you, but I don't feel very much like the *adultiest* adult. I'm 37 and I helped raise my siblings and my mother, and yet I still don't feel grown enough to be the one in charge. Or maybe that's not true. I feel grown up enough, I just don't want the responsibility. But here we are. I think God sent me to this family for a reason.

I used to roll my eyes when I'd see people get emotional about missing their moms who had died years ago. I'd think to myself "What a baby. They must just be weak." I thought it'd be different for me.

And yet, after three years I still find that it hits me out of the blue. It'll hurt like no time at all has passed. When I hear "The Little Drummer Boy" at Christmas (it was her favorite Christmas song). When I see a pineapple upside-down cake. When someone gives me leftovers to take home. When someone hugs my kids. The hugging the kids one gets me every time. I cry writing it and reading it too.

In those moments, the pain is as sharp as it ever was, and the missing her is just as real.

You're not weak for missing your mom, even if she was a shit. You're not a baby for yearning for the love she gave you, even if that love was toxic. It's a foundational love found nowhere else. A special love that's hard to say goodbye to. The hard truth is, you can't love someone without risking the pain of loss. They are two sides of the same coin. Anything worth having will be dreadfully painful to lose. That's just the way life is.

"Grief and love are conjoined, you don't get one without the other."

-Jandy Nelson


So, I'm thankful for this pain. It's proof of how deeply I was touched by this imperfect love.

It still feels strange that the world keeps going though. Something so monumental has changed, and yet the world doesn't even pause. Don't people know a great light has gone out? Can't they see me floating up here?

But the world doesn't stop. People go about their day. They're not altered the way you are. It doesn't mean they didn't love her (those that knew her). They just haven't lost the same love you lost.

And everyone grieves differently. There are no rules to grieving. There's no timeline, no right or wrong way to do it, no set standard to how you "should" behave.

The hardest part of grieving is allowing yourself to feel it all. Allowing yourself to go through the entire process to its completion. It's fucking terrifying. Grief isn't fun. And in our society, we tend to run from pain. Please don't run from this.

You probably want to avoid grief altogether or rush through it. You might think it's selfish to be sad. That it's time to move on. Maybe you're worried your grief makes others uncomfortable. Or it just plain sucks and you don't want to feel it.

In our world, strength is applauded. That means being tough, stifling the urge to cry, and being stoic. But confronting and feeling your grief is the strongest thing you can do. It takes real gumption. Some people will tell you it's okay to fall apart as long as you pick yourself back up as fast as you can. People can be confused by how long it's taking you to work through your grief. Don't let that alter your course. Do what's right for you.

If you're feeling weird about it, speak up. You might tell friends or family "Listen, I'm gonna be sad for a while. It's going to take me a bit to work through this. You don't need to try to cheer me up and you don't need to dull your happiness to make me more comfortable. I'm going to be okay. I just need time to work through this."

Sometimes the act of saying it out loud helps dissipate the tension, imagined or real. Bring the issues to light and grieve how you need to. They may not even realize they're trying to "fix" you until you say something. It's human nature to want to "fix it".

There's much to learn from grief, so don't rush it. I don't say this to keep you stuck in your grief either. I don't want you to be grieving any longer than you need to. I simply want to ensure you grieve completely, in order to heal as completely as you can.

Now that we've established how different the pain of losing your mom is, and that it's okay to grieve, let's get into the nitty-gritty about how to grieve, shall we?

# Shock

Victims of 911 or Hiroshima experienced shock. It's safe to say the level of shock they experienced is much higher than any shock you or I have encountered. The bigger the tragedy, the bigger the shock. Regardless of whether the death came suddenly or after a long illness, the body has emergency response systems in place to protect you. That's what shock is, a self-protection mechanism.

When you're in a car accident, you'll experience shock to keep you from feeling physical pain. In the same way, when you experience severe emotional pain, the body is designed to put you in shock to protect you.

Sometimes it lasts a day or two, sometimes it is prolonged. In severe cases, the shock can be difficult to bring yourself out of without outside help. That's when you might need to seek a therapist or your faith or a physician. It's okay to need help. Sometimes it's out of your hands. Asking for help is a beautiful way to care for yourself.

Shock is usually phase one in grieving. For most people, shock starts as a feeling of numbness or disbelief. You might feel like this can't be real. She can't be gone. Someone is playing a trick on you or this is a bad dream. You may not even feel sad yet, because part of you is unable to believe it.

As the days and weeks go by, the shock will start to ease. Usually in small doses. Suddenly the sadness will overwhelm you for a few minutes, and then, just as suddenly, you'll feel nothing again. Think of it like a pressure-release valve. There's so much grief inside so your body just lets a little bit out at a time. Just enough to help you get through it slowly, so it doesn't overwhelm you all at once.

It's kind of a genius design if you think about it. You're not broken for not falling apart. You're in shock. Have you ever seen someone appear unfeeling at a funeral? Maybe it was you. You're sitting there wondering why you aren't crying, what's wrong with you? Will others think you're a monster? Have you considered others as monsters for the same reason?

Remember shock is real. And it lasts for varying amounts of time for everyone. Don't judge others for the way they grieve, and don't judge yourself. Allow yourself and others to feel what they feel for as long as they need to feel it.

Shock is a normal reaction to grief. The bigger the grief, the bigger the shock. It will eventually wear off and the sadness will kick in. That is unless you slip into denial first.

# Denial

♥

> "If I don't accept it, then I don't have to feel it.
> And I don't want to feel it."

Denial is a close friend of shock. It's another way to keep the pain from feeling real. It can also be considered a self-protection mechanism. But this one isn't as healthy for you. This is you trying to deny how you feel to protect yourself. Denial is a lie. It's a desperate attempt to avoid confronting the truth. Truth that hurts, so you're trying to hide from it.

You might fool yourself into thinking you're handling this so well when really, you're too afraid to handle it at all. Denial doesn't make you look strong. If you look closer, you'll see the scared child inside of you who doesn't want to look at his or her pain.

You might be afraid to break down. Afraid that if you start crying you won't be able to stop. Afraid to feel the pain that you know is there. But it's waiting to be felt. It's going to keep waiting and it will never go away until you look at it.

You're trying to stop the natural progression of your grief. It's meant to flow out. You're trying to stuff it down against its will. And that can cause problems. The longer you deny it, the bigger the pain gets. This is like the pressure-release valve being clogged up by a dirty sock. If you don't let it out, it'll explode. And usually in ways you don't want it to. In ways that cause more pain and damage than would have happened if you'd just surrendered to it.

It's not easy to admit, or even realize that you're in denial sometimes. And even when you do, it's scary to allow yourself to feel. That's why you're in denial in the first place. One of my siblings went into a bit of denial when our mom died. In some ways, he's felt it and dealt with it, but in others, he's still running from it. For example, he won't go inside my mom's house. I think he knows it'll hurt to be there without her, and he wants to avoid that pain. That's not to say he hasn't hurt deeply. He has. But in trying to staunch the flow, he's refusing to sit with parts of his grief.

And I can't tell him to deal with it. Because I know we all grieve at our own pace. But I also know the dangers of avoiding that grief.

Denial can have a whole grab bag of side effects. Sometimes it can turn into substance abuse. People use drugs or alcohol to numb the sensations they're trying not to feel. It's a way to keep those unwanted feelings down below the surface where they don't have to look at them.

Other times it can look like working hard. But a sudden obsession with work can be an attempt to become too busy to feel. A desire to do anything they can to distract themselves.

Sometimes denial can just make you depressed, angry, or all around unpredictable in mood. That pressure is building, and it has to come out somewhere. It might feel like something is wrong, but you aren't sure what. You might be sad while pretending not to be. Doesn't that sound exhausting? It is.

Some even say that unresolved grief can manifest in physical ways. You can get sick, get injured, or have unexplained pain. The body has its ways to make you listen when you don't want to. It's like an alarm blaring. "Listen!" it says.

The problem with grief in general, is that no one teaches you how to deal with it. It's only natural that some might turn to substances to avoid it. Especially if that is how your parents dealt with unwanted feelings. You can't know what no one ever taught you. But I'm trying to teach you now. It's never too late to learn how to grieve. Your mom will probably not be the last person you grieve. It's important to know how it works and how to navigate it in a healthier way.

Once again, have compassion for yourself if any of this sounds like you. And have compassion for others if you notice it in them. You can't force anyone to let go of denial before they're ready. We're all allowed to grieve in our own way.

If you've been in denial, and you're ready, work your way through it. Start to sit with the truth. The longer the denial, the harder it will be to face. So do your best to be honest with yourself. She's gone. Sit with that.

You have a choice in this. You get to choose what to do with your grief. Do you die along with them? Do you pretend to live a half-life while hiding from yourself and your pain? Or do you face the pain, and live authentically through it?

Through your grief, you let the dead go but also bring them closer. It's letting go of one version of them, and gaining another. That's how you get through the pain.

Give yourself some time. Find a nice quiet space where you feel safe. Think of your mom and what she meant to you. Allow yourself to feel the truth of it. Take deep breaths. Cry. Rage. I know it hurts. I know. But we must all face the truth to move forward.

It can help to write it down. So, I'd like you to write another letter to your mom. Please don't skip this step. There's power in writing it down. It allows you to go deeper and see things more clearly.

For this letter, I want you to tell her what it means that she's gone. Like before, I'll go first.

*Dear Mom,*

*You're gone. And that sucks. Because you're gone, my kids never get to see their GG again. They don't get the chance to get to know you as older versions of themselves. They can't stop by to see you and show you when they get a driver's license. They can't come by to try to sell you fundraiser popcorn. They have lost the chance to have you in their lives.*

*You miss out on being with them too. Maybe you can see them. I hope you can. I hope you can see how awesome they're turning out. But you're not here. Not here here.*

*Because you're gone, I can't ever have the chance to have a better relationship with you. It will never be better than it was, because you're gone.*

*There will be no new memories to make. No more funny GG stories. I guess there's no more of your drama either. You were a lot of drama. There will be no more requests for gas station booze.*

*No more picking you up to take you to the grocery store. I'll never see the phone ring with your name on the caller ID. And there will be no more early morning calls from you to check on me or to tell me the latest gossip about the family.*

*I won't hear your voice or feel your arms around me. I can't call you to ask how many days before Thanksgiving to take the turkey out of the freezer or how we're related to someone. I can't call to tell you some strange person knew who I was, and I had no idea who they were. I'd describe them to you and you'd guess who it was and remind me how I knew them.*

*But I also won't have to take care of you anymore. I won't have to watch you hurt yourself. I won't have to watch others hurt as you hurt yourself. I guess you saved my kids from seeing any more of that too.*

*You'll never get the chance to get better, to figure it out. You'll never get to do any of the things you didn't get to. Or go to any of the places you hadn't seen yet. We only took you to the ocean that one time. And you said, "I feel like I've wasted my whole life". I thought you'd be excited to see it. Instead, you were sad that you'd waited so long.*

*Because you're gone, I don't have a mom anymore. I don't go to your house for the holidays. The kids don't trick or treat from you. You'd always load them up with the good stuff.*

*Now that you're gone, the snack cupboard is empty. And the house you kept so clean, is in disarray. No music is pouring out the front door when I pull up. You aren't out in the yard with the lawn mower or planting a garden.*

*You're gone, and you took all that was you, with you when you left. And that really sucks. It really does.*

*Because you're gone, my heart hurts. It hurts in a way that I'm not sure will ever fully heal.*

*But because you're gone, I'm writing this book. A book that can make the world a tiny bit better. That can help people heal just a little. So some good is coming from your leaving. I've learned a lot from your leaving. But I still miss you so much.*

*Love Always,*
*Holly*

That's a lot to confront. It hurts. It's so fucking sad. I wish a lot of those things weren't true. And yet they are. That's real life. Facing the ugly truth is better than living a pretty lie. Even if that truth hurts for a while.

Your mom wouldn't want you to live in denial. When you deny the pain, you deny her. Think about that. When you're trying to shove this sadness down, you're shoving the memories of her down. Don't you want to remember her? Remembering her keeps her alive. And there are so many great things to remember.

That's the biggest reason to deal with denial, so you can stop denying the love. And when you stop denying, you might find you're a little mad.

# Anger

♥

> "I never met my mom. She died when I was a baby. Having not experienced this type of relationship it only makes me envious of even the bad ones. These at least have the potential to be repaired." – Tracy Theisen Hastings

Sometimes in our anger, we lose perspective. We forget it could have been much worse. Some people have it much, much worse. I'm sure many people are reading this who have experienced things much harder than an alcoholic mom.

But it's not a competition. We all have pain. It just looks different than others. We all hurt and we're all trying to heal. Sometimes that pain may look like anger.

Anger can take a couple of different forms. Sometimes we get angry in an attempt to avoid sadness. It's easier to be mad than to have to sit in sadness. Other times, we're just left with a lot of things to be mad about.

I spent most of my life feeling mad at my mom. I loved her, but boy I was mad. It was hard to see the good she brought me through all the things I was mad about. You might feel mad at your mom. For what she did, or didn't do while alive. Or maybe you're mad at her for dying.

You might be mad at yourself. You might be mad at death, at the food industry, at God, at life in general.

Anger is just as natural as all the other emotions. But I find it doesn't last as long unless you're trying to hold onto it.

People find it easier to be mad than to be sad. They find it easier to be mad than afraid too. Death is scary, and so is confronting the feelings you have around it.

Anger can be another form of denial to be tricked by. Take a look at your anger and ask yourself if you're mad, or if you're using it as a shield from your sadness.

Other times, you have every right to be mad at your mom. Maybe she fucked up big time. Maybe she let you down or caused real pain.

Maybe you feel like your mom abandoned you in dying. Maybe you feel like she didn't take care of herself or you. Maybe you're mad at her for the person she was or the person she could never be.

Maybe you're raging at God for taking her from you. You feel like it was too soon. You didn't get enough time with her.

Your anger can be directed at yourself, or you might find you're lashing out at others. Wanting to blame others for this loss isn't unheard of, but it's a sign that you're not dealing with it, and instead you're trying to push it off onto someone else.

It's okay to be angry for a little while. But eventually, you need to deal with the anger.

Start there. Permission to be upset. Permission to be mad as hell.

Now that you've done that, let's take a look at why you're mad. Time for another letter. Get your paper out.

I'm sure you're getting the hang of this by now. Here's mine.


*Dear Mom,*

*I'm really mad at you. I'm mostly mad because you were an alcoholic. Because you wouldn't or couldn't quit no matter how many times I begged, bartered, or guilted you.*

*I'm mad that you made me watch you hurt yourself. You made me watch you slip away. Not just your health, but who you were. It was slipping away. You stopped caring. You stopped fighting. You stopped wanting to be here.*

*I'm mad that you gave up and died. I'm mad that you drank a fucking shooter in the hospital once you finally went. I'm so mad that you didn't go to the hospital sooner.*

*I'm mad that you allowed yourself to have a life you hated. You could have loved your life. There was so much you could have done differently. And I think alcohol had a big part in that. It stole your life from you, your dreams, and you let it.*

*I'm mad that you became this shell of a person I didn't respect and didn't want to be like. I'm mad that we didn't have a better relationship. I'm mad that you aren't here watching your grandkids grow up and helping me potty train this three-year-old. You potty trained the rest of them. You left the job unfinished.*

*I'm mad at you because much of your misery, and mine, was your fault. You created the life you lived and chose the people you allowed in it. We went through what we went through because you allowed it. You allowed your husband to beat you up and stayed. You chose to stay. For way too long. You chose the wrong men. You chose other people thinking it would fill a void within you when you should have been choosing yourself all along.*

*I wanted you to do what was right for you. I'm mad that I never get to see what you could have been if you'd done the work and healed. I'm mad that I never got a better role model. I could be further along now instead of still trudging through this healing work you left me with.*

*I'm mad that I didn't get to have a good mother-daughter relationship. That you couldn't just drive to my house to see the kids. I'm mad for all the times I was ashamed to know you while you were drunk in public.*

*I'm mad that you said I wasn't your pretty daughter, I was your smart daughter. I'm mad that you didn't get me. You didn't understand me. You didn't fight for me and our relationship when I stopped fighting for it. You let me let you go. I was the kid. I didn't know.*

*I'm mad that you let me be the grown-up in the family far sooner than I ever wanted to be. I'm mad that I had so much responsibility thrust onto me. I'm mad that I was taking care of you when you should have been taking care of me.*

*I'm mad at you for leaving this all unhealed. For leaving. For quitting. For dying. For the way you lived. For the way I lived. I've been so mad for so long.*

*Love,*
*Holly*

I was so mad at her. Forever. For my whole life. That's a heavy burden to bear. It's heavy to hold onto all that anger.

When she was dying, I sat on her bed in the hospital with her and I told her, "I'm so tired of being mad at you. I just want you to get better." But she didn't. And so, I was left with that anger, and no one here to be mad at anymore.

My anger didn't change anything. It didn't fix her. Being angry never made anything better. It probably made things a lot worse. Not just afterward, but while she was still here too.

My being angry was never going to be enough to get her to change. Because she didn't want to change. Or she didn't have the tools to change.

The ugly truth here is that I wasted a lot of time being mad at her, instead of just having a relationship with the person she was. I didn't have to agree with her choices. But they were hers. The choices belonged to her, and that's what she decided to do with them.

I robbed myself of a relationship with her. She didn't rob me. But sometimes, you can only walk with the light you have to see by. You don't know better. And you have to allow that to be okay.

I couldn't have done it any other way because I didn't know any other way. And maybe that's what's true for my mom. She couldn't have done it any other way, because she didn't know of any either.

I can see why I was, or am, mad. I had some pretty damn good reasons for being mad. But I can also see now that it doesn't change anything.

Holding onto anger just means you get to keep it. And it's heavy. So, let it go.

How do you let it go? It's not a one-size-fits-all here. But through this book, we're going to try a few different ways to let go of this pain.

For anger, sometimes it's as simple as being tired of being mad. Sometimes it's recognizing that it doesn't, and it won't, change anything. Sometimes it's taking a kickboxing class, breaking something, shouting at her headstone, or talking to a counselor.

I've found healing in the simple (yet powerful) act of writing it down. I can look at it more clearly on paper. I can accept that it's the truth. It's okay that it made me mad, but I can't change it. So, it's time to surrender to the truth of what is. We're angry at what didn't come to pass. It's what hurt us. It's the part of the journey we didn't like. It's refusing to accept that this is how it all turned out. Knowing it could have turned out differently if only... if only the people we love weren't those people. If only our journey wasn't our journey. If only we could change things.

But we can't change things. This is it. What's come to pass, has come to pass. Even though it wasn't perfect, this story is yours. This story is mine. It made us who we are today. And that's not so bad.

Once we give anger its due, we surrender to sadness.

# Sadness

♥

"Grief is like the ocean, it comes in waves ebbing and flowing. Sometimes it is overwhelming. All we can do is learn to swim." – Vicki Harrison

The emotion we try not to feel. The feeling under all the other feelings of loss. The pit of grief.

Even though we don't like to feel sad, sadness isn't the enemy. All sadness, at its root, is love. It's proof that you've lost something wonderful that was worth having. Your sadness will ebb and flow. It'll grow big and shrink small.

It's okay to be sad. I give you permission to be sad. Be as sad as you want. Say, "Hello sadness. I see you. Let's sit together here." Allow your sadness it's due. That is the only way to get through it. Any other way is just pretending.

You have to feel the sadness to get through it. And sadness will still come back to visit once in a while, even after you accept it and deal with it. But each time sadness returns, she'll be smaller and gentler.

Sadness is an emotion that'll stick with you forever around your mom. To really love someone, means being sad when they're gone.

The sadness might start strong. It might even be viewed as depression. Maybe you'll need to work with a counselor to get it under control or move past it. Or perhaps this book will help get you through it.

In desperate situations, you might need the help of an antidepressant. I wouldn't take an anti-depressant for too long though, otherwise, you're letting the medication do the grief work for you. And that's just another form of denial. But I'm not a doctor, so talk to your healthcare provider about what's right for you.

Depression feels like isolation, like despair. Like you're all alone with this heavy grief and you don't know how to set it down. I want you to know you're not alone. Many people have felt what you're feeling. *You are not alone.*

I find there is comfort in that statement. I'm not alone. You're doing this with me. I'm here with you. I'm holding your hand through this. I'm cheering you on. We're getting through this together.

Your mom is no longer here physically. And that's one of the saddest things you'll ever feel—no matter what kind of relationship you had with her. Your life is now changed forever.

Sadness and depression can become harmful when they linger *too* long. They can take over your life, and affect the lives of your spouse, your kids, your coworkers, and everyone you know.

So it's important to know when you need help.

Help can look like any of the following:

- Therapy.

- Talking to your local priest, rabbi, or spiritual leader.

- Going to a healing retreat.

- Meditation.

- Reading.

- Alone time to process your sadness.

- Bubble baths and self-care.

- Talking to a friend you trust.

- Getting outside in nature.

- Spending time with your kids or loved ones.

- Journaling.

Sadness is a big one. It's important to pay attention to your sadness and try not to be consumed by it. Death is tricky. It will try to keep you from remembering to live. It will keep you from being conscious of all that you have left.

This next task might end up being closely linked to the last. Often the reasons we're sad, are close to the reasons we're mad. But let's bring them to the light anyway. Get out your pen and paper, and let's talk to Mom again.

*Dear Mom,*

*I miss you. I've never missed you like this before. I can remember missing you some as a child if I was away from you. But never like this. I miss you with an ache that wrenches my guts and my heart. I miss you in a way that I know there will be no relief from. Until I find you again beyond this life.*

*At the bare bones of it, I'm sad that you're not here. Having you here wasn't always the best time. But not having you here is worse. Life is such a jerk for doing this to me. Why couldn't I see this before?*

*I'm sad that this is the end of our story. I want all stories to have happy endings. The fact that I'm working through all this is a form of a happy ending I suppose. But it's not the fairy tale happy ending I would have preferred. But we all know that's not typically how life works out.*

*I'm sad that I don't get to have the experience of knowing you as a healed woman. As a woman who was as strong as she claimed to be. I'm sad that this is the end for you. That you leave all your dreams undone.*

*I'm sad that my kids had to lose you too. They loved and love you so much. They cherish their GG memories. I'm sad that they won't be able to have any more. I'm sad that they're growing up without grandparents on my side.*

*I'm sad that your house doesn't feel the same. It feels empty of the energy you brought into it. It feels empty of your spunk. It just feels like a house now, instead of a home. I'm sad that the snack cupboard is empty.*

*I'm sad that I couldn't see the role I played in making our relationship harder until after you were gone. I'm sad that we can't have a do-over. I'm sad that I was so mean to you. I'm sad that I didn't force you to go to the hospital sooner.*

*I'm sad that my siblings don't have you when they need you. And I'm sad for the grief they've had to endure. I'm sad they lost you too.*

*I'm sad that I didn't take the opportunity to ask you for advice or ask more about your life. Of course, I wish I knew more of you now. I'm sad that you never wrote anything down. That I don't have any pieces of you left that I can hold in my hands.*

*I'm sad that you aren't here to spice up the holidays. Yes, you were a hot mess half the time. But it always made for a good story. And me and the siblings have shared many laughs over the years about your antics. We still do.*

*It makes me sad to know you aren't here giving your blessings to others. You can't take food to your brothers anymore. You can't give a friend your dress that they liked. Your blessings have left with you. And that's sad.*

*Your laugh is gone. Your smile is gone. Your loud music and your funny dance (that my sister can recreate perfectly).*

*You're not here to do something ridiculous that makes me roll my eyes but secretly entertains me.*

*You were the only you in this whole world. And I'm sad that you aren't here anymore.*

*Love Always,*
*Holly*

While your mom is gone, she isn't the only person you'll ever love. There is still so much life and so much love to be had. Take a look around and remember all the reasons you have to live. All the blessings you still have.

Your mom would want you to be happy. And even in cases where you don't agree, you owe it to yourself and your loved ones not to stay stuck in this phase. Be kind to yourself and give sadness it's due. But don't stay there. Don't allow sadness to suck you down and keep you from living. Death is part of life and you have to remember the life part when death is so raw.

That's why there's a second writing challenge to this section. I want you to write to your mom and tell her all the good stuff that still exists in your life. Write down everything you're thankful for that's still in your life.

Here we go.

*Dear Mom,*

*Hi. I'm still sad. But I can see all the reasons I have to try to remember the good stuff. You wouldn't want me to be sad forever. Ultimately, you always wanted the best for me. And I want the best for me too. It's hard to want the sunshine when you feel like you need the rain.*

*But I'm going to do this anyway. These are all the things I'm thankful for even though you aren't here. And I hope you're watching over me, and helping me nurture these things and add to this list.*

- *I have amazing kids.*

- *I get to be a better mom than you were to me.*

- *I have an amazing and supportive partner who allows me to live my dreams.*

- *I have amazing siblings and family members still here.*

- *I still get to celebrate holidays.*

- *I am healthy, as is my family.*

- *There is so much joy still in the world.*

- *Funny movies and funny people.*

- *Big puddles to drive through and splash water up along the sides of my car.*

- *My work.*

- *My talents.*

- *My ability to help others.*

- *My podcast.*

- *My blog.*

- *My books.*

- *My dear wonderful friends who are always supporting me.*

- *My lessons. Each lesson has taught me something.*

- *Warm drinks.*

- *Travel.*

- *Love.*

*It kind of hurts to say that I have so many blessings even though you're gone. It makes me feel a little guilty. But I think we have an obligation to see the light even in the darkness. That's the whole point of living. There will be hard stuff and dark stuff, but the light is what makes it all worth it.*

*I think in a way I honor your memory by living the best life I can, by taking what I learned from you and making my life better and brighter.*

*I'll never not miss you. But I'm thankful for all the reasons I still have
to smile and enjoy my life. I love you, Mom.*

*Love Always,*
*Holly*

Remember all the reasons you still have to live. All the many reasons
why life is still this magnificent thing. This thing is worth living. Life
is undoubtedly hard. But even with all its challenges, it's worth it.
Because even on the darkest days, there's always something worth
living life for.

# Your Mom Wasn't Perfect

♥

As you've gone through some of these writing challenges, you might be confronting the very real fact that your mom wasn't perfect. Far from it in most cases. There were things you wish were different. Me too.

It feels as if my mom didn't have the tools needed to raise me. I needed her to be wiser than I was, but that wasn't the case. Maybe I was sent to her though. She wasn't sent to me. That's an interesting way to think about it.

The reality of the situation is that I do blame her for many of the problems I have or had. I don't care if this was the divine way it was meant to work out. I've got scars! And that sucks!

I blame things that go wrong for me on her. I see how her actions have spilled over into my own. Like I'm drinking from a dirty river. It flows down from upstream and I can't seem to clean it enough before it finds its way into my cup. Some days I don't even realize I'm drinking from the cup. That's how passing down traits works. We aren't even conscious of it sometimes.

They say generational trauma is a real thing you can inherit. It's easy to spot in the mother-daughter dynamic. But they say it can be genetically handed down through multiple generations. That means some of your "crap" isn't even yours.

Which leads me to Mom-Blaming. We could Generation-Blame, but it's hard to blame the people you don't see. It's much easier to blame the person most closely linked to your biggest beliefs in life and the biggest traumas you encountered.

Maybe you don't trust your judgment because your mom always told you that you were wrong or that you didn't know what you were talking about. We don't consider that maybe that was a generational thing that was passed down to her too. Instead, you just see that she did this to you.

Maybe you weren't loved enough. You miss the fact that she wasn't either. But it's her you blame.

Some wounds in your life are your mother's fault. What happened to you might be ugly. You might have every right to blame her. Sometimes that's the cold, hard, truth. But another truth is this: carrying around the weight of all that blame, doesn't make it easier to walk. The past is heavy. It's time to set it down.

Here comes another writing challenge. Mine will be long. I encourage you to get it all out like I'm about to do. I want you to tell your mom all the things you blame her for. Everything you can remember. Anything you wish you hadn't inherited from her, or things she put you through. Try not to feel guilty as you go through this. It's important to bring the issues to the light. You can't heal what you're hiding. Ready, set, go.

*Mom,*

*I find that I have a lot of blame in my heart. I don't like that it's there, but it's true. So, I'm going to get it all out here and now. And hopefully, that'll help me lay it to rest.*

*My main blame is your drinking. It's my main sad and mad too. It was your biggest demon. A demon you didn't protect me from. You wouldn't stop. You didn't stop. My life would have been better if you had.*

*Remember the time I put the empty 40 bottle in the fire? You were having a big party out in the yard around the campfire. I was cleaning up a bit. I saw that empty bottle, I put the lid on it and I tossed it in the fire. I was only 10 or so. A few minutes later, the bottle exploded and a piece of glass hit me in the cheek. I still have that crescent moon scar on my cheek.*

*Maybe if you'd been sober you would have seen what I was doing and stopped me. Or maybe there wouldn't have been a bottle there for me to throw in the fire in the first place.*

*You and Dad would get drunk and fight all the time. You guys weren't violent to each other that I can recall. But I saw yelling. I saw cheating. I saw leaving. While the woman in me doesn't blame you for leaving, I find that I blame you for always finding the wrong man for you. I guess it's good that you did in this case since that's how I came to be here, but your taste in men has been questionable. And I find that mine hasn't been much better at times.*

*I've done to my kids what you did to me. I've broken up homes because I didn't know I was picking the wrong man. I've caused my children pain because you caused the pain in me. You passed it on.*

*You could never be on your own either. That's something I looked at from a financial perspective and tried not to copy. You'd always be with a man so he could financially support you (and us kids). While that's kind of admirable, I never saw you do it on your own. And while I've become sometimes hyper-independent as a way to prevent that in my own life, it's as if I'm still you deep down. I still have the urge to rely on a man or believe that I can't make it on my own. Even though outwardly that wouldn't be what you'd see by looking at me.*

*I never saw you be alone. I never saw you just be Gina. Who was she? Gina, alone. I have no idea. And you probably didn't either. And I never saw it before now, but I've never been alone either. I didn't choose men to care for me, but I had one constantly all the time anyway. Because I've never had the strength or the desire to stand on my own two feet. I find that I hate that. If I'm ever single again, I vow to change that.*

*Even though you always had a man, I'm not sure you believed good men existed. You had very little faith in them. You looked for evidence all the time that they couldn't be trusted. You looked for reasons to be upset at them. You had no faith that they weren't doing something shady. And here I am in my life doing the same thing. I'm looking for reasons not to trust men. I'm looking for evidence that I'm being tricked or mistreated.*

*I hate that too.*

*I hate how you made me feel about myself. You made me think I wasn't pretty. I wonder if you'd remember when it happened. It was on a day when I was feeling down on myself. In trying to cheer me up you said, "Holly, you're the smart sister. Your sister is the pretty sister." I remember feeling stunned that you actually said that to me.*

*Looking back, I can see that you were just trying to show me what you perceived as my greatest strength, but it hurt. It felt like you were telling me I was ugly, that I'd never be beautiful so I might as well lean into being smart. It stuck with me for so long.*

*You didn't think of yourself as smart. So you were so impressed that I was. You loved that I got good grades and didn't need help with homework and naturally excelled. But that wasn't all I was. I wish you could have seen that.*

*I wasn't part of the beautiful club. All the women in my family were beautiful. And I felt as though I was on the outside of that circle. I don't think you knew those words would affect me like they did. I don't think you were trying to hurt me. But I'd hear them every time I looked in the mirror, every time I went somewhere with my sister. So much so that I would worry my boyfriends would think, "Damn, I picked the wrong sister" when they'd meet her.*

*Because I didn't feel beautiful on the inside, I honestly wasn't much to look at on the outside. It's only in the learning to love myself that I've started to evolve on the outside. You didn't believe I was beautiful, so I didn't. It took decades to feel like I was good enough. Not everyone is going to be a supermodel, but everyone should feel beautiful in their own skin. We're all our own unique kind of beautiful. Like artwork.*

*You hurt my sister too in saying that too. She felt like she wasn't smart. So she didn't even try to be. And that was a disservice to her. Because she has a beautiful brain.*

*You made us feel jealous of each other. It made us rivals. I love my sister and I want the very best for her. I want her to be better than me. But that comment made us feel less than one another in some way. You and your twin were constantly fighting and competing. It was being passed to us. She and I have talked a lot about this. I like to think we've done a lot of work on this, but the roots run deep. It can take a long time to get each one out of the ground.*

*As a mother, your words had great power. Maybe since your mom left when you were young you didn't know that. But you had to. I'm sure there were things your dad or stepmoms said that stuck with you over the years.*

*There was another comment like that first one. You'd been drinking. My sister and I were getting ready to go somewhere. You came into the bathroom where we were doing our makeup. You looked us over, smiled,* and said we looked good but we "couldn't have held a candle" to you in your day. We were like, "Uh, thanks Mom".

You were trying to make yourself feel good. Trying to go back in time to relive your glory days. At our expense. That was unkind. You weren't aging gracefully because of all your drinking and you were struggling with that. But you should have found more about yourself than just a pretty woman. There was more in there than that. But you built your whole identity around how you looked and when the looks faded, so did your sense of self.

I blame you for making me watch that too. Like a fire slowly burning out. Strong and beautiful. Those were the only words I ever heard you call yourself.

I blame you for my relationship with money. If you had two dollars in your pocket you'd have to spend it. There was no such thing as saving. You knew nothing about money really, and so that's what you taught me, nothing.

I inherited some of your money behavior. I'm still trying to work my way out of it.

I also blame you for embarrassing me too. One time when I was a busser at The Chuck Wagon Steak House, you and your friends came into the bar. You were all drunk before you got there. The bartender served you one beer and then cut you off.

And you weren't just sitting there quietly. You were loud. And we lived in a small town. Everyone knew you were my mom. Everyone looked at me with pity in their eyes. My boss knew, my coworkers knew, and the other customers knew.

I wanted to crawl under one of the tables. You were oblivious, just having a good time. I get that you weren't trying to embarrass me. But you were a mess and you refused to see yourself that way. You just kept drinking to cover it up.

*I blame you for staying with the first Dave so long. For allowing us to watch you get the crap knocked out of you. Do I blame women for finding themselves in abusive relationships? Absolutely not. Maybe you didn't know it would turn out that way. But I blame you for staying. I blame you for allowing it to continue and allowing us to see it.*

*That trait, thank God, wasn't passed down to me. I'd never allow a man to hit me. Ever. But you gave me the pain from seeing it. From watching you go through it.*

*I know people love their abusers. I think you loved Dave more than you'd ever loved anyone. So maybe it felt impossible to leave. But I can't forget. Like the time Dave slammed your head into the corner of the wall. That ugly scar on your forehead never let you, or me, forget. And some scars run deeper than the physical ones.*

*Or the time he tossed you down the porch steps. You fought back, which I admire. But that wasn't a war you were going to win with your fists. The only way to win that war was with your legs, using them to walk out of there and never look back. Which you did eventually do. But at what cost first? How many precious years were wasted before you left?*

*You passed me your ability to leave. The only problem is, I put up with much less than you ever did. In fact, after any small fight, I'm planning our breakup in my head. I think I blame you because I'm a flight risk. I don't have a single example of love working out, of it standing the test of time. Not one. And so my solution is always, "I guess this is the end. Let's break up."*

*Maybe that has served me in the past. But it's hard to say for sure.*

*I blame you for robbing me of my childhood. I didn't get to be a kid. I didn't get to play. Playing feels foreign to me. I have to try to have fun. I almost have to force myself to have fun. I always had to be serious. I was the one in charge, always on alert, taking care of everyone around me.*

*It wasn't safe to dream. I wanted to be a writer. I'm 37 and I'm just now getting to be. Because that wasn't a safe job. I needed stability and security. I needed to be the opposite of you. So I went into the medical field. And I stayed there much longer than I should have. Because I was terrified to chase my dreams.*

*Because of you, chaotic people feel like home. The people I immediately like, I shouldn't like. Sometimes good people who are "normal" make me feel, so uncomfortable that I can barely stand to be around them. I don't know how to act or how to relate to them.*

*And still, it's the drinking that is under all of these other blames. I know I already said it, but I am having such a hard time letting it go. It connects to every other blame I have for you. People quit drinking all the time. They go to meetings and get sobriety coins. They change their lives.*

*But you didn't. I remember asking you to for as long as I can remember. After you died, I found a letter in your room. It was from me when I was 16. It said you should love us enough to quit drinking for us.*

*I remember you tried a few times. I remember you shaking too much to drink a cup of coffee. I remember you throwing up in the bathroom as part of the withdrawals too.*

*You were a serious alcoholic. So the withdrawals were serious. Over a few days, the shaking would subside and you'd be able to eat breakfast. I remember thinking how white your eyes looked. I'd never seen them so white.*

*But you'd eventually go back to drinking every time. I didn't understand. I watched you ruin yourself. I watched you slowly kill yourself. You gave all your power away. You couldn't even drive yourself to the grocery store.*

*As kids, we couldn't have friends over unless their parents drank too. Otherwise, their parents wouldn't let them stay. Or, not a second time anyway.*

*You wouldn't get better. Not for yourself and not for us. Even when you were yellow. I asked you what you were thinking about after the doctors had come to talk to us at the hospital (once we finally got you in there). You said, "I guess I should have stopped drinking".*

*I later found out that your brother snuck some Fireball shooters into the hospital for you. Why would you drink them at this stage? Knowing what you were up against? Knowing you were literally fighting for your life?*

*I blame you for giving up. For not trying harder. All those years talking about how you were the "rock" and how you were so strong, and yet you gave up in the end. You didn't fight.*

*I blame you for making my life harder than it had to be. Less beautiful than it had to be.*

*Love,*
*Holly*

That was a long letter for me. I have a lot of blame in my heart. I've been carrying it around for a long time. It felt good to get some of that off my chest. It felt very emotional too. Take a moment if you need it. You can always come back to this after processing some of it.

Now that you've gotten the blame off your chest, let's set that aside for a minute. I want to zoom out a bit and look at some of the stereotypes for women in general.

I'm not a die-hard feminist, but I am a realist. And some of the standards set for women are just unrealistic. They leave us feeling bad about other women and about ourselves.

In our society, women are held to ridiculous standards. I'd say they're getting better. But there are still some that influence the way we think about women. Moms especially.

Standards like all women should fit a beauty standard made up by someone else. Supermodel looks. Don't get me wrong, those super-models are beautiful, but so are other women. I love the color pink, but that doesn't mean the color turquoise isn't beautiful too. There are different kinds of beautiful.

Women also have to be sweet and loving. Don't lose your temper now, or you'll be accused of acting "crazy". A woman should be smart, but not too smart. She should be honest, faithful, kind, and perfect. She should put the needs of everyone else before her own needs or she's selfish.

And for moms, the standards are even more rigid. They can work, but only if they still spend time with the kids, help with their home-work, cook meals, clean the house, make the doctor's appointments, and of course put the needs of everyone else before their own needs.

Doesn't that sound crazy when we put it down on paper? You want a mom to pay attention to you but not smother you. You want her to cook good food but blame her for your weight because you refused to eat anything healthy and she was trying to make you happy so she made you the foods you liked.

We forget that our moms are human women. They are people. People with their own lives, who have suffered their own traumas (often worse than yours) and are just doing their best to survive life.

Thinking about that from the perspective of a mom myself feels awful! I don't want to be held to some standard of perfection. I don't want my kids to be mad at me for every tiny thing I fell short of. I really am trying my best. But what if it's not good enough?

Guess what? In some ways, it won't be. We know more than our moms knew. They grew up in a different time. They didn't get to talk about their traumas or work on them. They just had to survive. That was life.

Women now have breathing space. We can now see how these things affect us and we get a chance to change them. Our moms didn't have that.

Maybe that's part of why our moms were so fucked up. And why they couldn't be perfect for us. They never got a chance to heal, they never even knew they were broken.

Consider what your mom's life was like, and what she went through. Zoom out. See her as a woman, not just as your mom. Is it fair to blame her for everything you're blaming her for? Would you blame your best friend for some of these things?

It's an interesting question to pose. I want you to pose this question as you write another letter to your mom.

Some of the things you blame her for are fair. But some of them might not be. This is what came up for me:

*Mom,*

*Is it fair for me to blame you for all these things? I don't know. That's such a complicated question. It's hard to say what's fair and what's not. Some things you could have done better. But maybe you couldn't have because you didn't know any better. Can I blame you for something you didn't know?*

*I do still blame you for the drinking. You knew it was a problem. But you were surrounded by drunk people. I think it would have been really hard for you. It was hard for you. I'll give you that. But you should have done it for us, and for yourself.*

*People quit all the time. You could have too. But you didn't.*

*I guess I don't really blame you for your taste in men. You were given no examples of good men. Neither was I. I can't blame you when I haven't done much better than you did. We were both given poor examples. You did a little better than your parents. I did a little better than you. I guess that's the way it goes.*

*I do think it's fair to hold you accountable for staying when the first Dave hit you though. You had to know it wasn't good for us. You had to know that. Maybe you thought it wouldn't happen again, or that you could fix him. Maybe you thought it was your fault. I never heard you say anything was your fault ever in life. But that doesn't mean you weren't thinking it.*

*It makes me sad to imagine that might have been what you were thinking. A man hitting you is never your fault. We all have responsibility for our own actions. Maybe it was your fault to choose a man who was toxic to you, but his actions were his own.*

*As for money, when you were growing up, women were being allowed to have their own credit cards for the FIRST time in history. So of course they didn't know how money worked. I can't blame you for your lack of financial knowledge any more than I could blame you for not teaching me Chinese. You can't teach what you don't know.*

*You never meant to make me feel ugly. You were trying to show me what was great about me. My brain is still one of the greatest things about me. I love that about myself. But I'm more than that. I don't want to fit into any more boxes of what I "am".*

*You didn't have a mom. Your mom left you with an abusive and alcoholic dad. You never left us. No matter what. I know you were just trying to be a better mom than your mom was. The bar was low there. All you had to do to beat that was stay.*

*I won't go through every little thing I blamed you for in the last letter. But I'll say this, there is a difference between blame and accountability. A lot of your behavior wasn't your fault. But it was your job to grow and learn. And there was so much more you could have done.*

*I find that through this, I don't blame you anymore. I understand you a little better. And I recognize that some of it wasn't your fault. But I also think you could have done better. Is it your fault you had the life you did? Is it my fault I have the life I have?*

*There isn't much point in saying what's fair and what's not. This is the reality. What does it matter if it's fair? Life isn't meant to be fair. We're meant to meet our challenges and learn and grow.*

*You may have learned and grown some. But you could have done more. I don't feel mad about that anymore. It's like the pressure has been released. And all that's left is just the truth.*

*This is our story. And all I can do now is grow through my challenges. You left me with some hurdles to climb. But I've decided to climb them. I will not surrender.*

*I'm sorry your life was hard. I'm sorry you didn't do more to change it. I see you though. And I love you.*

*Love,*
*Holly*

I love that. There is a difference between blame and accountability. It's okay to recognize things could have been better. Blame is when you're still mad about it. It's when you're raging against the reality of what is. It's wishing it had been different.

But it couldn't have been different. It wasn't different. What happened happened. And there is no going back to rewrite the story. All you can do now is move forward.

My mom would be horrified to see me airing all her dirty laundry here. But in order to stop repeating history, we have to be honest about the history. I'm doing that openly and honestly here for you in hopes that it will help you do the same.

As mothers, we won't always do or say the right thing. We're trying to help with the tools we have. And things don't always go according to plan. I remember asking my mom once, "If you grew up with an alcoholic dad, and hated drinking, how did you become an alcoholic?" She said, "You don't plan for it to happen. You just drink one time with some friends. And it's fun, so you do it again. And you want to keep having fun so you keep doing it. And the next thing you know, you can't go without it or you're shaking and throwing up. So you keep drinking."

We don't always plan for these things to happen. But we can learn to plan better. What kind of life do you want to have? And what can you do to get there? Are the habits you have now taking you closer to that life, or further away?

Only you can change your life. We each have a responsibility to learn and grow. You won't be perfect just like your mom wasn't perfect. But you can be just a little better than she was. You can learn from her mistakes. And in doing so, you can make your kids a little better than you were.

# The Pain of Regret

♥

There are always regrets when someone dies. The regret of not doing enough, doing too much, not spending more time together, not being kinder. The list will likely be long.

It's easy to be hard on yourself for what you didn't know at the time. Looking back things tend to look so much clearer. It's suddenly easy to see how you could have done it better. You wonder how things might have turned out differently if you had.

You probably didn't have time to do and say everything you needed to. Even if you knew it was coming, there's never enough time. And there's no way for you to know the pain that's coming or how it will affect you.

You can't know until you're there. You can't experience something until you do.

There are big things I regret, and small things too. Let's take a look at these. This was probably the hardest letter to write to my mom, but don't let that stop you. It was also the most beneficial I think. The hard things are important. So take a deep breath and tell your mom what you regret.

*Dear Mom,*

*I think I might have a lot of regrets. And I hate that I do. But here they are.*

*I regret that I couldn't see you as a woman. I only saw my mom. I didn't see that you were a whole person completely separate from me. A woman who was trying the best you knew how. You'd had your heart broken, you'd had everything taken from you again and again. I saw you only as my mom, the one that put us in this situation. I didn't give you any grace. I regret that. I wish I could have seen you as a human being. But I didn't. That must have felt awful. To be judged so harshly by your own child, that you lived and breathed for.*

*I find that I also regret that I took you for granted. All the things you used to do for me. You babysat all my kids. You loved them. You let me live with you after a breakup. You fucking MARRIED for stability for us kids. So we would have a place to sleep. The men you chose weren't always the best, but you didn't know what love was. You would have broken yourself over and over if it meant doing so for us. You never abandoned us like your mom did to you. You'd never do that to us, even if it meant keeping us in poor situations with you. It was your way of being better than your mom before you. By not abandoning us.*

*I wasn't kind to you a lot of the time, especially in the recent years before you died. I was a jerk to you as a teen. I was a jerk to you as an adult. Unless you were doing something for me, I was a jerk. I was snotty. I was a jerk towards the end because I was so sick of you drinking.*

*I regret being embarrassed by you. Every time you'd show up, I'd be torn between glad and embarrassed. But you showed up. I wonder if you knew I was embarrassed?*

*I so regret not spending more time with you. The older I got, the less time I'd spend with you. Before you died, I'd rarely come over anymore. I didn't want to see what you were doing to yourself. I wanted to forget. I wanted the distance.*

Part of me even has regret for writing this book. For showing the world all the ways you weren't perfect. For being so hard on you. You hated to look bad, physically or otherwise. And I'm pretty sure this book shows all the bad.

I regret not hugging you more. I regret not saving your voicemails or birthday cards from you. I regret that I didn't take you on more trips and that I tied you down to your house with my kids. Maybe you would have been working or doing more with your life.

I regret a lot of things.

I think I regret giving up on you too. I gave up on you long before you died. Maybe you just needed someone to believe you could do it. That someone shouldn't be your child. But maybe it could have been.

I regret that I wouldn't let myself laugh with you. I was determined not to find joy in the madness you had created. Even if you were funny when you were drunk I didn't want to laugh. It was like saying it was okay for you to be this way. But I regret it now, not finding the joy in the little moments when I could have.

There was some beauty still to be found in the mess. But I didn't want to find it. I refused it. Because I wanted things to be different and I was mad that they weren't.

I regret that I didn't talk to you more. I didn't ask your advice or let you tell me more about your life. It's all gone now. Those memories are gone forever. You never wrote them down. I never asked for them. And now they're gone with you. I can't undo that.

I regret that I didn't love you for the mom that you were to me. I was too busy raging against what you weren't. I wish I could have seen all that you were.

I wish I could go back and change things. But the sad truth is that I can't. You can't understand the lesson until you go through it, until you learn it. And sometimes it's just too late.

*Love,*
*Holly*

Okay, now it's your turn. Write this letter to your mom. It'll be hard. But it needs to be said. Say the things you wish you could take back, the things you wish you could do over.

Don't worry if you cry. I cried a lot while writing this. I've cried so many tears over this whole book.

It's time to own up to the ways you may have fallen short too. We're doing that thing again where we're taking an honest look at things.

The truth is ugly sometimes. But it always beats a lie.

# *Forgiveness*

♥

> "She wasn't there. But I never thought it was
> because she didn't want to be." – Tina Hileman

Things don't always work out the way we'd planned. Not in our lives, and not in the lives of our moms. Sometimes good intentions turn into bad decisions. Sometimes the best they could do wasn't good enough.

It's time to forgive. Forgiveness doesn't mean you're saying what happened was okay. It means you understand. It means you don't want to carry all this heaviness with you.

Forgiveness is for you. It's the path forward.

This writing challenge may be hard. You might still feel some resistance. That's okay. It's not easy to let these things go. If you need to revisit the previous writing challenges for a second, or even a third time, you can. Rework any of these challenges until you feel better.

I want you to know your anger at her isn't punishing her anymore, she's gone. You weren't even really punishing her when she was here. It was always punishing you. The anger has always been loaded in your own heavy bags to carry. No one else even knew you had luggage.

It's time to forgive your mom. Forgive her for the person she couldn't be. Forgive her for the person she was. Understand that she could only have been the person she was. The story is written, you can't go back and change it.

Get out your paper and write this letter to your mom.

I'll get it started.

*Mom,*

*I forgive you. I forgive you for your past and your patterns. They carried onto me, but you didn't mean for them to. You didn't know how your actions would affect me. You were just trying to do the best you could.*

*I forgive you for making me feel unpretty. You were trying to show me how smart I was, and that is cool. I am smart. I forgive you for making me think I wasn't beautiful. I am beautiful. And through this lesson, I've learned that your face is the least important thing about you. I'm so much more than pretty because of you.*

*I forgive you for not healing the traumas you had. You didn't even know what trauma was. And I think you were afraid to look at it. You were trying to survive your life. You needed to keep moving. And that sometimes meant ignoring reality.*

*I forgive you for your taste in men. You couldn't have known better. And, it did get better with the last husband, so maybe you were learning. I wish you could have seen that not all men are bad. There are some wonderful men in the world. You hated them all towards the end. I forgive you for teaching me not to trust.*

*I forgive you for not being perfect. Even on the days you were doing good, it was never enough. I put unrealistic expectations on your shoulders. That was unkind of me. Women aren't meant to be perfect. Humans aren't meant to be perfect.*

*I forgive you for not knowing what you were doing. It's not like anyone taught you. You were trying to do better than your parents did before you. You did by the way. You did better than they did. I'm proud of you for doing better than they did. The bar was set low, and that's not your fault.*

*I forgive you for not chasing your dreams. I'm sad for you that you didn't chase them. It seems like something I wouldn't need to forgive, but it set the tone for the first part of my life. You were never safe to chase your dreams, and neither was I. Once I started chasing my dreams, I was so sad that you'd never know the magic of it. You missed out on that.*

*One of the hardest things to forgive you for is the drinking. It's so hard to forgive the thing that wounded me the most. But forgiveness doesn't mean I think it's okay. It just means I understand. It means I'm not going to be mad about it anymore.*

*You were broken in this way. There were so many parts of your life that hurt, and you were trying to numb the pain with alcohol. You were trying to find your joy in the beer can. The answer was never there, but you didn't know where else it could be, so you kept looking there.*

*You were surrounded by it. It was in every part of your family, friends, and identity. You felt trapped by it. Maybe you were trapped. And I think you only thought you were hurting yourself. You didn't see what you were doing to me. The booze whispered in your ear that we were going to be just fine. Have another sip.*

*I forgive you for being broken. Even if your brokenness broke me.*

*And lastly, I forgive you for quitting on life. This is the hardest of all. You gave up when I didn't want you to. But I should know by now you were going to do whatever you wanted to do, to hell with the consequences.*

*You had a hard life. From birth to death. You were fighting through it the whole way. While you may have made some of your own problems, you couldn't see your way out of them.*

*In the end, you were tired. You didn't have anything left to give. How can I tell you not to go? How can I expect you to keep fighting? I forgive you for leaving.*

*In the end, we all get to choose. We choose to do the cancer treatment, or not. We choose to fight, or surrender. We all get a choice. I didn't respect your choice. I was mad at your choice. But now I see that allowing you to live life your way, and leave your way, is the greatest gift of all.*

*I hope to never try to take away someone's right to choose how they want to do this whole living and dying thing.*

*I hope you feel my forgiveness where you are. I hope it heals whatever wounds my anger created for you. I hope you see me, seeing you.*

*Love always,*
*Holly*

> "I don't have kids of my own. I realized at a young age that my mom was finding her way through life just like I am. She didn't get to go through life before kids. She was three short years on her own before we came along. Realizing this is when I decided to respect the sacrifices of her younger self for us. I felt the need to give her grace because as a parent, she was just a kid too. Just trying to find her way through life like I am." – Kristen Fernau

I love that quote because it allows us a glimpse into our mothers as more than our mothers. As human beings. And usually young human beings who had no idea what life was about yet, much less how to teach that to someone else. In a way, we grew up together.

As hard as you might have been on your mom, I would imagine you've been just as hard, if not more so, on yourself now that she's gone.

Forgiveness isn't just about forgiving others, it's about forgiving yourself. As I've said before, there was no way for you to have known until you went through the thing that taught you.

We didn't do it all perfectly. We could have handled things differently. But we didn't. Maybe there's no way we could have. And now the story is set in stone.

Sometimes I wish I could have been a different person back then. But I didn't know what I didn't know. I hadn't learned it yet. We waste so much time holding onto the regrets of what we did or didn't do. These bags are heavy too.

But it's time to give yourself grace like you gave your mom. Like you'll one day want your children to give to you.

This time you're writing a letter to yourself. Here we go.

*Dear Me,*

*Hi. Weird to talk to you like this. I just wanted you to know that I forgive you.*

*There was no way for you (me) to know it would turn out this way. We were young and inexperienced. Things played out the only way they could have. There's no way to have made a different ending with the information we had available.*

*I forgive myself because I was making the best choices for myself in those moments with the knowledge and experience I'd had at that point. That's how life works. You make choices based on what you know at that moment and what you think will be best or hurt the least.*

*I forgive myself for forgetting all my mom did for me. I got so wrapped up in my own life and the things I thought she did wrong that I lost track of all the sacrifices she made to help me get this far. I forgot to be grateful.*

*I forgive myself for focusing on the bad. I was dealing with some heavy stuff. I didn't know how to do that. I was doing the best I could to protect myself. There were a lot of great things about my mom. And I'm glad I've been given the perspective to remember them now.*

*I forgive myself for being a brat. I was unkind. I think it's the easiest to be mean to the person you know will love you no matter what. No matter what I did or said, she would love me and forgive me. I wish she would have stopped me, and told me I couldn't talk to her like that. But she didn't. Mostly she just let me be a butt.*

*As grown as I thought I was, I didn't realize that had to have hurt her so much. I forgive myself for that. And I will try to remember this lesson so I won't repeat it with others.*

*I forgive myself for not seeing that I had a mom that loved me and showed up. She wanted to be in my life. She wanted to spend time with me. Not everyone has that. She wasn't perfect, but she loved me.*

*I forgive myself for not knowing that time would run out. I've tortured myself thinking if I had been a better daughter to her at the end, maybe she wouldn't have been so depressed, she wouldn't have waited to go to the hospital, she would have fought for her life. I'll never know.*

*But I do know, that her mental health was her responsibility. And her life was in the state it was because she let it get that way. Maybe she didn't know better but it's still the truth. And the human I was at that point was just trying to protect myself. I was doing the only thing I could think of to minimize the pain I was experiencing. I didn't know she was almost out of time. And so I have to forgive myself for that.*

*I forgive myself for writing this book and airing all her dirty laundry. She would have hated it. But I needed to do this. I needed to confront all these details and demons so I could heal and move forward. I wrote it so I could help others do the same. I want us to all do better for our kids. I wrote this so I could learn to love my mom. Really love her. The good, the bad, and the ugly. All of her, instead of just the pieces.*

*I forgive myself for the choices I made when I couldn't have known any better.*

*Love,*
*Me*

Take a deep breath and sit with that. Do you feel lighter? I do. The bags are lighter now. They're getting easier to carry.

# The Future She Didn't Get

♥

Our moms don't have a future. There are no more memories to be made. And that is such a devastating reality.

My mom will never see my kids grow. She'll never get to see them graduate high school. She won't get to see them have kids of their own. She never even got to see my youngest get bigger. He was still so little.

It's not just that she doesn't get to have them, they won't get to have her either. They won't get to know her any more than they already do. And those memories are already starting to fade.

They won't get to call grandma for advice or questions. They won't get to ask her how to make her spaghetti sauce. They won't get to experience holidays with her.

There are grandkids she didn't get to meet even once. She didn't get to see all these amazing humans carrying on her line.

She won't get to see the new house I buy. She didn't get to read the first book I wrote. Or the second. She doesn't get to see the human I grow into. I wasn't done growing yet.

She didn't get to know the man I love. Or meet my daughter's first boyfriend. Or see my son driving.

She didn't get to grow old. She's missing out on so much.

She won't be here come Thanksgiving. The kids can't trick or treat from her anymore. She won't be here at Christmas.

Part of mourning is mourning the future she doesn't get to have. The future you don't get to have, and the future your kids will never have with her either.

There are so many branches to this tree of healing. Just when you think you've fallen from the sky and hit every single one on the way down, another sneaky one slaps you in the face.

That's what grieving the future feels like. Adjusting to a new normal that doesn't include your mom. The first Mother's Day without her was terrible. The first of any of the holidays. It feels like something is missing. It feels sad. Even when everyone else is there and you're still so grateful to have them. You can't help but feel a little lonely.

My mom was a hot mess at holidays. She'd be drunk by the time we made it to her house to trick or treat. But she bought the best candy. She gave everyone a ton of it. And she always opened a sucker or two for the smaller kids. She knew we would try to keep as much candy away from them as possible so she'd pass it out while she could. They loved going to her house on Halloween.

The same could be said for Thanksgiving and Christmas. We'd always have a big dinner. She'd insist on hosting it. She'd also insist on doing most of the cooking. And by the end of the day, she'd be mad at all of us for not helping. And she'd be drunk by dinner time. Haha.

But she was still fun most of the day. She'd make sure everyone had everything they needed. Everyone had a plate (except her because she'd be full from the drinking by then). Everyone was welcome in her home for food. Even if she couldn't remember who they were and that they'd attended holiday dinners every year for a decade.

I already mentioned the snack cupboard. The one she'd fill with sugary delicious snacks. When she would babysit, the kids all knew where it was. They'd ask if they could have a snack and my mom would point them to the snack cupboard. When we'd come by to pop in, she'd tell the kids to grab something from the snack cupboard before they left.

The first time I took my youngest son to the house after my mom had passed, he asked my stepdad if he could have a snack. He told him to see what was in there. He came back from the kitchen with some snack he'd never seen before. He asked my son, "Where'd you get that?" My son pointed to the cupboard (that my stepdad didn't know about) - "From the snack cupboard."

But Dave didn't know he was supposed to fill the cupboard. It was never his job. Soon the snacks ran out. My son went to grab a snack, and the cupboard was empty. No more snacks. Such a silly little thing to cry over. But it symbolizes who she was in a way. She always had food for anyone who stopped by. That was her love language. She wanted to feed you.

One day I was having a hard time thinking about the empty snack cupboard, and my sister said, "Holly, did you notice you recreated the snack cupboard at your house?" She pointed to my little cupboard in the kitchen. The one that was the same size and shape as my mom's, that was filled with snacks. Where the kids all knew they could go to grab something to eat. I burst into tears.

I had no idea I had recreated the snack cupboard. So even if she isn't here to fill hers, there are always snacks to be had.

It's hard to let go of the future she won't get, that you won't get. It's so hard to confront the truth that this is real. She'll never get to be here again. Not in the way she was.

But all these things you miss, are part of why you love her so much. It's part of her greatness. Some of which you couldn't see before she was gone.

She doesn't get any more tomorrows. But she had a lot of yester-days.

# The Gifts Left Behind

"Mother, it's not a job but a lifestyle. Mothers like mine were mothers to everyone who needed it. And while sometimes it might have felt like she cared about me a little less than others because she would spread herself so thin doing everything she could to help others, it also proved that she was a good woman who never stopped trying to make the world a little bit better. My mother taught me patience, kindness, and most of all she taught me how to love, how to be loved, and how to deal with losing someone you loved as well. And even though she's gone, she is still teaching me how to manage, and showing me that there is nothing stronger than a parent's love for a child and a child's love for

a parent. I can't say my mom was the best mom
for everyone, but I can say she was the best mom
for me! I love you, Mom. I will always miss you.
Goodbye mother." – Justin Wilson

Your mother likely left you with more than you realize. She left you with the ways you exist in this world. Things like the snack cupboard. She left that to me without me noticing. Just like your mom has undoubtedly left good behind for you in her wake.

In some ways, we women become our mothers. When your mother is somewhat of a trainwreck that can be the last thing you want to hear. But we are all imperfect humans with both good and not-so-good qualities. Your mom was no different.

We've focused a lot on the bad stuff so far. But she left you good qualities too. And it's time for you to take stock of those as well.

I'd forgotten about these things before my mom died. They were always there in my brain. But I'd minimized those tabs. I wasn't looking at them. I was too focused on the pain, the wounds, my desire for her to be different, and my determination to be nothing like her.

It took her dying to bring the good stuff back. As you look at the wounds, the things you're angry about, the things you regret, you must also look at the things you're thankful to have experienced.

Most likely you'll need to take care of the anger and the wounds first. Once those are out of the way, you can focus on the good stuff. That's why this book is structured the way it is.

Get your pen and paper ready. It's time to tell your mom what you loved about her.

*Dear Mom,*

*I've been pretty hard on you so far. But as I work my way through my anger and disappointments, I see that that's not all there was. You were more than just the bad stuff. Nothing and no one is all one thing or another, we're all a combination of light and dark and good and bad. And now I'm seeing that with you.*

*I'd like to tell you what I loved about you. When I think back in time, I remember we always had a clean house and yard. You were a hard worker and you took pride in keeping things clean. You'd never wait for a man to mow the lawn, you just got out there and did it. Maybe in that small way, I got a glimpse of who "Gina" would have been without a man. That part of you would have been the same.*

*You had such a green thumb too. That helped the yard look great. You loved to plant and grow things. All summer you'd be in the backyard on your hands and knees, pulling weeds, planting, and harvesting. And when you had more veggies than you could eat, it gave you so much joy to hand them off to the people you knew.*

*Food was love, regardless of whether it was from the garden, food you'd cooked, or treats in the cabinet. It was your way of caring for everyone. The kids felt it, I felt it, your siblings felt it, even strangers meeting you for the first time could feel it. You nourished others in this way.*

*You always wanted to feed everyone. You'd make way too much for dinner so you could take leftovers to your brothers. You'd make ham and bean burritos for the men in our lives to freeze and take to work. I'd show up to drop the kids off and you'd have a BLT made for me or a fruit plate. It made you feel good. It was your love language.*

*Your house always felt like home even amid all the chaos. People inside it might be half drunk and crazy, but there was always love to be found. It felt like a place where you were always welcome, where you wouldn't be judged, where you could get a meal, rest on the couch, and always find a beer.*

*I remember you being the very best mom when we were sick. That was when you shined. When you were needed. You'd dote on us, turn on whatever we wanted to watch, make our food, leave glasses of water by the bed, and wait on us like a servant, or a very loving mom.*

*When I got older, being sick was one of the only times I'd allow you to care for me. I became obsessed with taking care of myself (trauma response). I'd rarely allow you or anyone else, to do anything for me. But I'd let you while I was sick. And you'd be so soft and kind, so motherly. That felt nice. Like being wrapped in love. I wish I hadn't pushed that love away so much.*

*Boy did you love us. Thinking of hitchhiking down the road with you doesn't make you think of love usually. But when I look at it now, that's what I can see it was for you. It was a determination to be better than your mother was, to never abandon us the way she'd abandoned you. Not even for a moment. You wanted us to know you loved us more than anything in this world. And you really did. You loved us more than anything, more than yourself.*

*You quit your job for me. I got pregnant halfway through college. I was one of the first people in our family to go to college. It was a big deal. When I found out I was pregnant, I was panicking. I thought I'd have to drop out. I was home for a visit and was trying to work up the courage to tell you. We were out running errands and you kept making comments that would scare me even more. We saw a mom and baby and you told me, "Don't even look at that baby until you're done with school." I thought I was going to die right there on the spot.*

*After a whole day of comments like this, I pulled into your friend's driveway to drop you off. I said, "Mom, I have to tell you something." You said, "What? You're pregnant?" And I burst into tears. You were so surprised. The look on your face, I'll never forget it. Although it seems like you could sense it. You somehow knew it.*

*I let it all out. I said I was afraid I'd have to quit school, that I was terrified, and I didn't mean for this to happen. And that's when my alcoholic mom, looked me in the eyes, and told me it was going to be okay. You said I wouldn't have to drop out, that you would quit your job and babysit. You said we'd figure it out. And I needed that. I needed to hear that and to have someone be there for me. You weren't always able to, or maybe I didn't let you, but that day, you were there for me. And I felt like it was going to be okay.*

*Maybe you let me down in life in some ways, but you were always there for me when I allowed you to be. You always had my back no matter what. I didn't know how lucky I was to have that. And I'll forever be grateful to you for it.*

*You ended up watching mine and my sister's kids over the years. You gave up your life and your free time so we could go out and make lives for ourselves. You potty-trained all those kids too. I've inherited another child in the last few years, and I despise potty training. I wish you were here to help me. Or to tell me how you made it look so easy. You even trained your cat to pee outside. You had a gift. Haha.*

*And you'd never lie. Sometimes you were brutally honest. But we never had to wonder how you felt or what you thought. You'd always say whatever was on your mind.*

*You were funny too. Not as funny as you thought you were, but funny. I'd probably never admit that if you hadn't died. So I guess you get the last laugh huh?*

*And even though I saw your weaknesses, you were strong. Life was hard on you. Hard in a real way. But for most of your years, you didn't crumble. Through every trauma or heartbreak, you'd say, "I'm a rock". You'd wipe away the tears and get back up.*

*You loved music. You'd always blast music. In the living room, in the car (my poor kid ears), in the yard, or anywhere you happened to be. You had The Beegees concert recorded on VHS. You would watch it over and over while singing along. I still know all the words to almost every song. If you ever had the chance to watch live music, you'd be in heaven. Your face would light up and you'd come alive.*

*You used to love to hike. You'd pack up some beers, and walk us through the woods to a place you called "the meadows". We'd spend a few hours just being there, and then we'd hike home. I'm going to try to find these meadows and put some of your ashes there. I think I can remember the way.*

*You didn't always have a car, so you'd walk everywhere. The lack of a car wouldn't stop you, you'd walk where you wanted to go. Because of that, you had the nicest legs on a woman I have ever seen. A guy once asked you how he could get his wife's legs to look like yours. You told him, "It's easy, just take away her car."*

*You were a beautiful woman. While that seems less important to me than your other qualities, it's still true. No one could deny what a beautiful woman you were. I think the beauty within made you more beautiful on the outside too.*

*The beauty within was one of your best qualities. You were a good person. If you only had two dollars to your name, and someone needed it, it was theirs. I'd buy you new clothes and you'd give them away to someone that liked them. It would drive me crazy. But you were a giver. Stuff was just stuff. People were more important. And you helped anyone you could.*

*You didn't give a damn what anyone thought. You were going to do whatever it was you wanted to do. That went for what you wanted to wear or say or how you wanted to behave too. And if someone didn't like it, that was too damn bad.*

*That reminds me of the story Uncle Mike told at your funeral. He said you were sitting on the corner dressed in "Gina clothes" (meaning something on the sexy side), drinking a beer, and a cop drove up. He said, "Ma'am, you can't solicit here." You looked him in the eyes and said, "I ain't soliciting, I'm waiting for my kids to get off the bus." Haha. You didn't give a damn what he thought either.*

*And you couldn't stay mad at anyone. There wasn't an offense big enough to keep you from forgiving them. You just didn't have it in you. It made you feel bad. You loved people. And I'm glad I can see now how much there was to love about you.*

*Lastly, you always had faith. You weren't the church type. You didn't feel right entering a church with beer in your system. But you knew God, and He knew you. I know that's where you are now. Put in a good word for me would ya?*

*Love you, Mom,*

*Holly*


That's a beautiful list. It made me cry to write it, but it made me smile too. There were so many wonderful things about her.

I hope your list was just as long, if not longer.

Now, this is a two-part exercise. You've recalled all the wonderful things about your mom. Now I want you to take a look at yourself, and see which of these qualities she passed on to you.

Our moms didn't just fuck us up, they gave us gifts too. Some of those gifts could only be given through her death. Some of those gifts you could only receive once she was gone. It's time we take a look at them.

*Dear Mom,*

*I feel lighter having admitted the good stuff about you. It feels nice to be looking at those things. I spent so long focusing on the bad stuff, and that didn't feel good inside of me.*

*Now I get to tell you the good things that I can see in me because of you.*

*I want to start by telling you I recently saw a quote that said something like "I want to cheer so loud for my kids that they never notice the people that don't cheer for them." You cheered loudly for me. And because of that, there was always this little river of worth running in me. I didn't always have access to it, or know it was there, but I've figured it out. Because you loved me, I was able to see how much I deserve love.*

*There were habits or traits you had that passed to me. And there were also things given to me in the process of losing you. Or gifts you gave me in the negative ways you chose to live. I didn't have to learn the lessons you lived out in front of me. But I want to start with the traits you had that passed to me.*

*The first of those was your desire to feed people. I have my own snack cupboard and always make too much for dinner. All my kid's friends know they can get in the fridge and find food anytime they're over. I invite people for dinner all the time. And I love when they want to take some leftovers with them.*

*For a long time, I didn't know I'd gotten this from you. Seems pretty obvious, but I was oblivious. It feels nice to see that it came from you.*

*You gave me the gift of being a hard worker. I won't claim to work as hard as you did, but I know I can when I need to. And there's something to be said about getting your hands dirty and cleaning your yard. I have no green thumb, but I do feel good having a clean yard. It feels nice to take something messy and make it clean.*

*I like to think you gave me the ability to make a house feel like a home. I make whatever house I'm in, feel like a home. It's the vibe I carry* with me and infuse into the space I'm in. Everyone always knows they're welcome.

I think my kids feel as loved and cared for when they're sick as I did. I make sure to get them what they need, dote on them, and tell them I love them. I think they feel cared for.

I like to think they feel loved in general. No offense, but hopefully I'm doing even better than you did with this. I guess you gave me that too. You gave me what you had and I took it and made it even better. I created even better, safer, more whole love for them.

My kids know I'm here for them no matter what. They know I have their back, just like you had mine. I'm there even when they're jerks, but I like to think I've created some healthier boundaries around the jerk behavior.

I inherited your honesty. Sometimes I'm a bit brutal with it too. But I'm glad to possess it. I love to be honest. Life is too short for lies.

I also got your sense of humor. Except I actually am as funny as I think I am. :)

You gave me your strength. Some of that was inherited from you, some of it was gained through living the life we lived, and a bit of it was made in losing you. But I am strong. I have the confidence that I can survive anything life throws at me. (That's not a challenge, God!)

Because of you, I'm a good human. I care about people. I want to help them. And I don't have the energy to hold a grudge. That part used to upset me. It would feel like I was allowing poor behavior. But I see a healthy way to forgive while also drawing a line in the sand to show what behavior isn't okay with me now.

You gave me your faith. Things don't always work out the way I want them to or think they should. But I've never doubted that God is with me. I've never been alone. Even in going through the painful stuff I went through as a kid, I was never alone.

*I feel like you gave me more profound things in dying. When you died, I saw all the dreams you'd never get to fulfill. So, in dying, you helped me to make my dreams a reality. I realized I only had one life to live. And I know what it looks like if I don't try. I quit my job to become a writer, speaker, and coach.*

*I was confronted with the reality that people die having never lived. Never trying the things they always dreamed about. So much of what you taught me was learned through what you didn't do in your life. Towards the end, you stopped living, stopped feeling the magic of life, and you stopped trying. You gave me the gift of knowing what that looked like. I won't do that in my own life.*

*As I look at you now, I can see how hard it was for you to love yourself. And that has given me the gift of learning to love myself. I wish you could have loved yourself as much as you needed to.*

*In going through this process, I've been given compassion for other people who have lost their moms. And I've learned to be compassionate to other humans who don't have it all figured out yet. You weren't trying to mess up, you were doing the best you could. And I think that's what most of us are trying to do. I have a little more grace for my fellow humans now.*

*You've given me the gift of seeing myself through your eyes. I couldn't see that while you were here. But now, now I can see how much you loved me. I can see who you thought I was, what you thought I was capable of, and how proud you were of me.*

*And lastly, you've shown me that I won't always be here for my kids. Someday I'll be gone. So I'm going to be the best mom I can be while I'm here. I'm going to leave behind memories, pictures, books I've written, and all kinds of things for them. I would never have known how important that was without losing you.*

*Thank you for all you gave me, both in life, and beyond.*

*Love,*
*Holly*

I recently did a writing challenge where I was asked to write an imaginary story where I got everything I needed from my parents growing up. Who did I become? In doing this challenge I could see a person that began my writing career sooner. I had more confidence. I loved myself more. I was further along in my journey.

But you know what else I realized? I wouldn't have been as compassionate. I wouldn't have the depth or understanding of others that I do now. I wouldn't be able to help people in this way. I'd be writing, but what would I write about? How shallow and meaningless my words would be. Isn't that interesting? I don't think I'd want to go without these warrior tools I've accumulated along the way. This strength I have, this unending desire to help others. I've been given gifts from the experiences I've had.

So even if there was a way to go back and make my mom perfect, I wouldn't. There are some beautiful things about me, and all because of who my mom was. She has contributed to more than my wounds. She contributed to my gifts as well. And that should be celebrated.

In reflecting on your own gifts, I hope you see that too. She gave you more than wounds, she gave you gifts, even if you have to look a little harder to see them.

The wounds weren't on purpose, and maybe the gifts weren't either, but it's nice to know they're there, balancing out the hard parts.

# Who You Are, Good & Bad

♥

At this point, you should be getting a glimpse at the whole picture. You should be forming this view of all the good and bad that has happened, and combining it into one. Neither good nor bad, but just real.

At some point, we have to stop thinking of our past in terms of good or bad. We have to change our perspective to more about what the reality was. Things aren't always good or bad, they just *are*. None of us are all good or all bad. We're a combination of all of it.

I like to think everything that happened has made me the human I am. Maybe that wasn't a good thing before I'd learned to love myself and see the gifts I'd been given through the hardships. But now I love the human I am. If I'm going to really and truly love myself, I have to honor the things that had to occur to make me into this human.

It's bizarre to consider all that had to happen for you to get to this moment. Not just with your parents, but with their parents before them. Your parents were raised a certain way for them to turn out how they did, and their parents were raised a certain way too.

All these generations that came before you. All the possible ways things could have worked out, and who you are is the combined effort of all those generations. This beautiful, perfectly imperfect soul that's reading this book right now.

You. You are the result of generations of love and loss and wounds and blessings. All combined and passed down until you came along. Now, not all of those things were wonderful, but they made you into the person you are today, didn't they?

And if there's some of it you don't want to pass on, guess what? You can change it. If it's drugs, if it's alcoholism, if it's cheating or lying or abuse. You are not powerless. Actually, you're more powerful than you realize.

It's as simple as deciding it's not what you want and making different choices than your parents made. Even if it's a big, hard thing. Don't underestimate the act of trying. That trying will be passed on too. And if you don't succeed, someone in line will. Because you took the first step. You created the pathway.

Every little decision our ancestors made affected us. Just like every decision you make, will influence your future line. It's up to you to decide what you want to leave behind.

Take a moment to look at the whole picture. Sit with it. This whole person you are. The good, the bad, and the in-between. How cool is it that you get to be this human?

# It's Okay to Miss Her

♥

I miss my mom all the time. I miss her early in the morning when she was the only one I knew who was awake. No matter what time I got up, she was already awake. Just knowing she was in her house, watching her lifetime movies and sipping her coffee (or beer), gave me a sense of comfort I hadn't realized I had.

I miss her calling me. I used to feel inconvenienced by the calls sometimes. But I miss having someone who just wanted to check up on me for no other reason than they loved me. Boy, do I wish she would call me now. I wouldn't be inconvenienced. I'd drop everything just to hear her voice.

I miss her rolling her eyes at me when I was being difficult (which was often). She would get so exasperated by me. She'd throw her hands up in the air and just say, "Never mind Holly". That always amused me.

I miss dropping my son off to her before work and her giving me a fruit plate or a BLT that she prepared for me. She knew I was coming and she wanted to feed me. No one else feeds me. No one else ever has a plate waiting for me, ever. It hurts to think about that. It gives me real pain. My heart squeezes and my eyes fill with tears at that thought.

I get to be that person for others now, but I sure miss having someone be that for me.

I miss her telling me all the drama happening in the family. She knew what was going on with everyone. She was like a bridge that connected us all. And she loved to gossip.

I miss her reminding me to call my siblings on their birthdays. I never forgot, but I liked that she did it anyway.

I miss the little things she'd do for the kids. The treats she'd buy them. I miss seeing the happiness on their faces when she'd give them to them.

I miss her cleaning. Any time we moved, she'd offer to deep clean the house before we moved in. Or, deep clean the place we were moving out of.

I miss her hugs. I didn't take her up on them often. I was too prideful, too stuck on taking care of myself to need or want a hug. But I miss them anyway.

I miss having a mom.

I miss my kids having a grandma.

I miss her love. Her imperfect love. I miss it.

But she's not completely gone. As hokey as it sounds, the people we love aren't ever really gone. I think they send us messages to let us know they're still with us.

I had two very real experiences happen to me concerning this.

The first experience was just a week or so after my mom passed away. I was hurting so much, And I had a dream. But it was more than a dream. It was real. The most vivid dream I've ever had. In my dream, I was sitting next to my mom and I was crying.

My mom looked good. She looked a little younger. Her face no longer carried all the heartache and struggle that it had while she was still here. Her wrinkles were smoothed, and she had a youthful appearance. More than that, she looked peaceful.

I was looking at her, devastated, chest caving inward, as she sat up tall and patiently next to me. It was like she was waiting for me to say something. I said, "I just miss you so much." And she looked at me with all that peace in her eyes and just nodded at me. Like she was saying "I know baby. But I'm okay."

I could tell she was okay. She was better now. She was as she should have been in life. It was more than a nod. It was her sending me this feeling. It felt like she couldn't say words, but she could say it in feeling.

When I woke up, I knew she had been there, that it had been real. She came to tell me she was okay now. We didn't need to worry about her anymore because she was okay now.

It was such a typical message for her to give me. She knew I was hurting and that I was tormenting myself over it. And she came to me to tell me she was okay. To ease some of my pain. To help me accept it.

I texted all my siblings to pass the message on. That's what she knew I'd do. That I'd want to make everyone else feel better too.

For a while after my mom died, my foundation was rocked. I began to worry about death. About leaving my kids behind. Every pain or issue sent me into a panic. What could it be? Was I dying? The idea of death had become more real and terrifying.

I was stressing out about everything, which wasn't normal for me at all. My typically calm demeanor had changed into anxiety that I could go at any time. One day, I was worrying about a pain I'd been having in my side. I was freaking out about it. I was in my car driving down the road. It was getting kind of chilly in the car, so I turned my AC off. A few seconds later, it came back on.

I thought maybe I hit it with my arm or something. So, I turned it back off again. A few seconds later it came back on. I stared at my dash. And I can explain it in no other way but to tell you I felt my mom's presence with me. That same peaceful presence I felt in my dream.

I turned it off again, and I said "Mom? Is that you?" Immediately the AC turned back on. I started crying. And laughing because I was crying. I tested it out a few more times. I said, "If you're Mom, don't turn the AC on." Nothing happened. It didn't turn on. Then I said, "Okay, if it's you, turn it on again." And on it went.

I asked if she was trying to tell me something. Pretty quickly I realized what it was. I was freaking out thinking I would die and leave my children as she had left us, and she was trying to tell me to stop worrying. She was trying to tell me I wasn't dying today and to chill out. I don't know how I knew that was the message. And maybe this whole thing sounds ridiculous to you, but it's my truth.

I think my mom was trying to help me in what little way she could from the other side. And it did help. After that experience, I calmed down. I stopped panicking over every little thing. I trusted that I was going to be okay. And slowly, the ground beneath me started to feel a little more solid.

Recently I read a book called 'Signs' by Laura Lynne Jackson. It's a book about the signs people we love give us from the other side when we're open to them. Laura Lynne Jackson is a well-known psychic.

I found the book to be very fascinating. And also comforting, to think they can talk to us from the other side. That they're sending us messages all the time. We often chalk it up to coincidence, but I don't think they are. Not really.

So, I suggest that book if it's something you'd be interested in.

Even if you don't believe in that kind of stuff, it doesn't hurt to consider it. If it gives you comfort, how can it be a bad thing?

The main point I'm getting at is that it's okay to miss your mom. She knows you miss her, and even though she can't physically be here with you, she's here with you in other ways.

Ways you might have already noticed, or ways you haven't paid attention to yet.

You're not a weak human like I used to think for missing your mom. You're a human that loved someone. And that's pretty amazing.

---

"I chose not to lose my mom, and instead to gain an angel. In my mind, my heart, and my life, she is still completely present to this day -and as wise, compassionate and stubborn as ever." – Kevin Hart

# *Acceptance*

♥

> "We talk about them, not because we are stuck or because we haven't moved on, but we talk about them because we are theirs, and they are ours, and no passage of time will ever change that." – Scribbles and Crumbs

This is where it all comes together. Acceptance. You can't cut through all the other emotions and go straight here. You have to go deep into the other emotions to move to real acceptance. It can't be faked.

But you have to move *through* all the uncomfortable stuff to get to the good part. It's tempting to get stuck in the grief or the denial, or even in the pain. Sometimes it's so dark there you can't see the path forward. But it's there. The path is there once you look for it.

It's hard to imagine acceptance when you're in the thick of the other stuff. It's hard to feel like you're ever going to be okay again. But you will.

It's going to take time but you will.

One of the most beautiful things about accepting the death of your mom is that it feels like meeting her for the first time. You might think you knew who your mom was, but I'd be willing to wager you hadn't fully realized it yet. Not when you started this book.

Death does give us some gifts. One of those gifts is perspective, though it's not easily attained. Through this process, you've gotten to know your mom in a way you didn't know you could. That's why the book is called "Hello Mom Goodbye".

You're saying goodbye to her, but you're also saying hello to the version of her you never saw before. And that's a beautiful gift.

This is the part where it starts to feel a little lighter, where you begin to see the whole truth of your experience. And for better or worse, who she was, and who you became as a result.

If this process has made you realize you don't like the human you've become, that's okay. You don't have to keep being that person. You get to be whoever you want to be. You can unlearn any of the bad patterns that came before you.

How? That's the question. In accepting the truth of your experience, you're part of the way there. Look at it with curiosity instead of hostility.

From there, the options are endless. You can see a counselor, an energy healer, a priest. You can start meditating, listening to podcasts, or reading books.

It doesn't matter where you start, just that you start. What are the things you want to unlearn?

Make a list. Write down every pattern you don't want to keep.

Then, beside it, write down how you might go about changing it. I'll give you my example.

Behaviors I don't want to keep:

- Lack of trust: I want to actively try to trust people. I want to work on myself. If I love myself, I will have faith that I can handle anything thrown at me. And I want to work on having more trustworthy people around me.

- Bad relationships: I should evaluate if a relationship is unhealthy (friends too). If it is, I need to let it go. If it can be worked on, then I can put effort into it. But I need to pick better people to have in my life and set better boundaries around what I'm willing to accept.

- Drinking: I should quit. It's not worth it. I don't need it. I read "How to Quit Drinking the Easy Way" by Allen Carr. That led me down a path of sobriety. I'm at a year now. I may keep that going, or I may dabble with drinking once in a while, but either way, I know I'm not my mother.

- Not chasing my dreams: I need to actively chase my dreams. Life is too short not to try, not to go for the things I was put on this earth for. That's why I quit my job to write my books (among other things).

- Not loving myself: I am worthy of love. I should love myself. There are so many wonderful things about me. I can meditate, take a self-love course, do affirmations, and tell myself "I love you" in the mirror.

Your list might be longer than that. That's okay.

My main advice is to keep trying new things until you find what works for you. If one thing doesn't fit, move on to another until you find the thing that works for you. Until you break the pattern you're trying to break.

You only get one life. Move forward and choose that life, instead of just reacting to what life throws at you. You can do this.

Another alternative might be that you've come to like who you are even more, likely because you now understand why you are the way you are and where it came from.

You've been given the chance to see more than just the hard stuff you've inherited, you now see the good stuff too.

I hope you can see that you are a beautiful combination of light and dark and contrasts. You were meant to go through the life you were given.

You were given gifts and strengths in going through it. Now you get to go into the world and use those gifts. Allow them to make you even better, and maybe even make the world a little better.

# I Wish I Could Tell You

♥

I sometimes catch myself thinking of the things my kids will miss when I'm the one who leaves this earth. It hurts my heart to think of them hurting, and missing me.

I think they'll miss talking to me, asking my advice, or hugging me. I give great hugs if I do say so myself. They'll miss being comforted by me. They'll miss my joy and my traditions.

The funny thing about missing things, like talking to me, is that they already know what I'd say. When you know someone that well, you can already hear the words in your head.

So this is my message for my own kids, for a time that is hopefully far from now:

*Kids,*

*Someday when you're wishing you could talk to me, write to me. And then imagine what I might say if I were still here. Because I am still here. And you knew me so very well, all my answers live within you. You know just what I would say.*

*"Mom, I'm really sad today. I wish I could talk to you. I had this terrible thing happen today. What would you say if you were here?*

*I'd say, "A bad day doesn't make a bad life. You're so strong. I know you're going to get through it. I'm watching you with a bowl of popcorn waiting to see how you handle it. I hope you handle it with humor. I hope you handle it with courage. I hope you handle it with love.*

*"You have all the tools you need. And you already know what to do. You just got used to me echoing out loud what you already know. And half the time you didn't take my advice anyway, so listen to your inner knowing and do what you were going to do anyway. Haha.*

*"I was so lucky to get to be your mom. You were blessed to have me too. But I was the truly lucky one. You already have everything you need. I could see that clearly in you. I believed it then and I believe it now even if you can't hear me say it anymore. I'm saying it here to remind you.*

*"I love you so much. You deserve love and happiness. Do what you need to do to get to that. Make hard choices if that's what your gut is telling you. You can do hard things. You can't screw up anything meant for you. And it's okay to make a complete mess of things. There hasn't been a mess made that couldn't be figured out.*

*"If you don't yet know what to do, it's because you're not supposed to do anything yet. You still have something to learn or see. Be patient and the answers will be revealed.*

*"The answers never came from me anyway. They came from God through me. And you still have a direct channel to him.*

*"Remember the time Cyri and I got lost on a hiking trail? I told her 'I don't want to bother God asking for directions.' She said, 'I'll ask! God, please get us out of here!' Ten seconds later a little old man walked up and showed us the way out, and conveniently disappeared somewhere along the way. God is listening. All you have to do is ask.*

*"And I'm here watching. I'm so excited to watch the rest of your life play out. To see all the amazing things you and your families do.*

*"When you miss my joy, be my joy. So often you were what caused the smile on my face anyway. When you miss my traditions, keep them. They belong to all of you now. When you miss my hugs, hug someone else. Give them the hug you wish you were getting. And you'll see how amazing it felt for me to give them to you.*

*"And know that my love still lives with you long after my skin suit is gone. It was just the container. The real magic couldn't be seen even when I was in front of you. Feel it. It's still there just like I am.*

*"And you may find books I send your way. Out of nowhere on hard days. You won't always have to read them since I know you don't all love reading. But the titles will say what needs to be said. And if you need more, it'll be inside the books. Those are the signs I'll send you to remind you of what I'm telling you now. I like to think I'll remind you with clouds too. I loved clouds. Big poofy beautiful ones. If I get a chance, I'll be sending those your way.*

*"Life is never going to be perfect. But you're the human you're meant to be, in the place you're meant to be. Trust yourself to do what you need to do. Be a good person and love yourself. You are all so worthy of love and you have everything you need within you. I love you more than you could ever imagine.*

*Love you always,*

*Mom"*

If you have kids, maybe you'd like to write a message for them to find someday too. I wish my mom had left something like that behind.

In considering this message I leave for my kids, I want to take my advice. I want to think about what she would say to me. So here's a final letter from this book. I'm writing it to her, but I'm also writing what I think she'd say to me too.

I'd love it if you wrote your version too.

*Mom,*

*I wish I could tell you I'm sorry we didn't have more, and better times. But I think you'd say we get the time we get and that's it. You'd say I was always so damn headstrong, I always thought I knew what to do, and I did. Often better than you did.*

*I acted as if I didn't need you. And you don't think I did. I needed you all along. I just wouldn't admit it. You knew I could do this life thing without you. You knew we all could.*

*You stuck with us after Dad died. Just long enough. You got us through the hard stuff and now you know we'll be okay.*

*You always had faith in us. And you'd roll your eyes when we'd meltdown and think the world was falling apart.*

*Sometimes I wish I could tell you that I'm mad at you. That I wish you would have done better. And I think you'd say you wish you would have too. That if you'd known it would have turned out this way, maybe you would have done things differently.*

*But you didn't know better. And life led you down a hard road. And you just did the best you could. I know you're sorry things were sometimes hard. I know you loved us and never meant to hurt us.*

*You were just doing the only thing you knew to do.*

*I wish I could tell you the kids miss you. Especially Atticus. He takes a new stuffed animal home from your house every time we go there. And I think you'd say you're watching them. That you miss them too but you're enjoying watching them grow.*

I'd say I'm a writer now and you'd say, it's about time. You always knew I'd write something someday. But you'd also be nervous for me and caution me not to rely too heavily on a man to take care of me while I write.

I'd tell you Annisa is job hopping trying to figure out what she wants to be when she grows up, and you'd say she was always the freest of us kids anyway. She'll find her way.

I'd tell you Justin is inventing things and fixing things and raising really smart kids. You won't be surprised at all. You'll say you visit them in their dreams and you got to meet Mabel after all.

Then I'd tell you Harry is now a business owner. Finally doing his own thing. You'd say he's been trying to boss you around for his whole life so it's good to see those leadership skills paying off. And that he's still your handsome boy.

You'd say "See, look at all of you doing fine without me." You might even roll your eyes as if we're being a little dramatic about it.

I'd tell you holidays aren't the same without you and you'd say, "Why because you finally have to do all the dishes instead of leaving it all for me?" Haha.

I do miss your hugs. But hugging my kids helps.

I do miss your traditions, but I try to keep them alive.

I didn't often ask for your advice because I didn't think you were qualified to give it. Sorry about that. But I can see that life actually taught you quite a bit and that maybe I didn't know as much as I thought I did. You'd be saying "Praise the Lord! She finally knows!"

I miss you. But I know you're with me, with us. Thank you, Mom, for doing the best you knew how to. Thank you for all the things you did do. And I'm sorry for the ways I wasn't a better daughter to you. Let's do better in the next life okay? Keep visiting us in our dreams and sending us signs. I love you, Mom.

*Love,*
*Holly*

I highly encourage you to try this out with your mom. You know her. You know what she'd say. And while I cried doing this, I also found myself smiling and laughing too. And that surprised me. Try out the list for your kids too. It can be something you leave behind for them. Tomorrow is not promised. And someday it'll be too late to write down the things you want them to know.

Please try this, and if you feel so called, shoot me an email and let me know if it helped:

write2holly@yahoo.com

I'd love to hear about it.

# It's Okay if You Don't Know What to Do

♥

At one point, your mom was in your shoes and she didn't know what to do. It's okay not to know what to do. There's not a roadmap, and each one of us is different. We have different needs and experiences. It will take us all a different amount of time to work through it.

Start with healing. One step at a time. And give yourself grace for not being perfect along the way.

You know, it's weird but every time I heal something in myself I feel as though I'm healing something for my mom too. Something she couldn't heal while she was alive. And that feels nice. It gives me comfort.

I quit drinking and I feel like I conquered this mountain that she just couldn't beat. I feel it clearing something in our family, something that was stuck. It clears a path for my kids moving forward, but it's like it cleared the path backward too.

No one knows what to do or how to grieve. That's why I wrote this book. To help.

You've done what you could if you followed the steps in this book. The rest is like a blank page. The future is calling, ready to be written. Go write it. I believe in you.

Printed in the USA
CPSIA information can be obtained
at www.ICGtesting.com
LVHW020546081224
798392LV00017B/806

*9 7 9 8 9 9 1 4 6 1 9 0 0 *